D1451164

MODERN WORLD LEADERS

Roh Moo Hyun

MODERN WORLD LEADERS

MODERN WORLD LEADERS

Roh Moo Hyun

Silvia Anne Sheafer

CHELSEA HOUSE
PUBLISHERS
An imprint of Infobase Publishing

Roh Moo Hyun

Copyright © 2009 by Infobase Publishing

All rights reserved. No part of this book may be reproduced or utilized in any form or by any means, electronic or mechanical, including photocopying, recording, or by any information storage or retrieval systems, without permission in writing from the publisher. For information, contact:

Chelsea House
An imprint of Infobase Publishing
132 West 31st Street
New York, NY 10001

Library of Congress Cataloging-in-Publication Data
Sheafer, Silvia Anne.
  President Roh Moo Hyun / Silvia Anne Sheafer.
    p. cm. — (Modern world leaders)
  Includes bibliographical references and index.
  ISBN 978-0-7910-9760-1 (hardcover)
  1. Roh, Moo Hyun, 1946- 2. Presidents—Korea (South)—Biography. 3. Korea (South)—
Politics and government—1988-2002. 4. Korea (South)—Politics and government—2002-
I. Title. II. Series.
  DS922.4642.N6.S54 2008
  951.9505092—dc22
    [B]   2008004878

Chelsea House books are available at special discounts when purchased in bulk quantities for businesses, associations, institutions, or sales promotions. Please call our Special Sales Department in New York at (212) 967-8800 or (800) 322-8755.

You can find Chelsea House on the World Wide Web at http://www.chelseahouse.com

Text design by Erik Lindstrom
Cover design by Takeshi Takahashi

Printed in the United States of America

Bang EJB 10 9 8 7 6 5 4 3 2 1

This book is printed on acid-free paper.

All links and Web addresses were checked and verified to be correct at the time of publication. Because of the dynamic nature of the Web, some addresses and links may have changed since publication and may no longer be valid.

TABLE OF CONTENTS

ARTHUR M. SCHLESINGER, JR.

On Leadership

L eadership, it may be said, is really what makes the world go round. Love no doubt smoothes the passage; but love is a private transaction between consenting adults. Leadership is a public transaction with history. The idea of leadership affirms the capacity of individuals to move, inspire, and mobilize masses of people so that they act together in pursuit of an end. Sometimes leadership serves good purposes, sometimes bad; but whether the end is benign or evil, great leaders are those men and women who leave their personal stamp on history.

Now, the very concept of leadership implies the proposition that individuals can make a difference. This proposition has never been universally accepted. From classical times to the present day, eminent thinkers have regarded individuals as no more than the agents and pawns of larger forces, whether the gods and goddesses of the ancient world or, in the modern era, race, class, nation, the dialectic, the will of the people, the spirit of the times, history itself. Against such forces, the individual dwindles into insignificance.

So contends the thesis of historical determinism. Tolstoy's great novel *War and Peace* offers a famous statement of the case. Why, Tolstoy asked, did millions of men in the Napoleonic Wars, denying their human feelings and their common sense, move back and forth across Europe slaughtering their fellows? "The war," Tolstoy answered, "was bound to happen simply because it was bound to happen." All prior history determined it. As for leaders, they, Tolstoy said, "are but the labels that serve to give a name to an end and, like labels, they have the least possible

6

connection with the event." The greater the leader, "the more conspicuous the inevitability and the predestination of every act he commits." The leader, said Tolstoy, is "the slave of history."

Determinism takes many forms. Marxism is the determinism of class. Nazism the determinism of race. But the idea of men and women as the slaves of history runs athwart the deepest human instincts. Rigid determinism abolishes the idea of human freedom—the assumption of free choice that underlies every move we make, every word we speak, every thought we think. It abolishes the idea of human responsibility, since it is manifestly unfair to reward or punish people for actions that are by definition beyond their control. No one can live consistently by any deterministic creed. The Marxist states prove this themselves by their extreme susceptibility to the cult of leadership.

More than that, history refutes the idea that individuals make no difference. In December 1931, a British politician crossing Fifth Avenue in New York City between 76th and 77th streets around 10:30 P.M. looked in the wrong direction and was knocked down by an automobile—a moment, he later recalled, of a man aghast, a world aglare: "I do not understand why I was not broken like an eggshell or squashed like a gooseberry." Fourteen months later an American politician, sitting in an open car in Miami, Florida, was fired on by an assassin; the man beside him was hit. Those who believe that individuals make no difference to history might well ponder whether the next two decades would have been the same had Mario Constasino's car killed Winston Churchill in 1931 and Giuseppe Zangara's bullet killed Franklin Roosevelt in 1933. Suppose, in addition, that Lenin had died of typhus in Siberia in 1895 and that Hitler had been killed on the western front in 1916. What would the twentieth century have looked like now?

For better or for worse, individuals do make a difference. "The notion that a people can run itself and its affairs anonymously," wrote the philosopher William James, "is now well known to be the silliest of absurdities. Mankind does nothing save through initiatives on the part of inventors, great or small, and imitation by the rest of us—these are the sole factors in human progress. Individuals of genius show the way, and set the patterns, which common people then adopt and follow."

Leadership, James suggests, means leadership in thought as well as in action. In the long run, leaders in thought may well make the greater difference to the world. "The ideas of economists and political philosophers, both when they are right and when they are wrong," wrote John Maynard Keynes, "are more powerful than is commonly understood. Indeed the world is ruled by little else. Practical men, who believe themselves to be quite exempt from any intellectual influences, are usually the slaves of some defunct economist. . . . The power of vested interests is vastly exaggerated compared with the gradual encroachment of ideas."

But, as Woodrow Wilson once said, "Those only are leaders of men, in the general eye, who lead in action. . . . It is at their hands that new thought gets its translation into the crude language of deeds." Leaders in thought often invent in solitude and obscurity, leaving to later generations the tasks of imitation. Leaders in action—the leaders portrayed in this series—have to be effective in their own time.

And they cannot be effective by themselves. They must act in response to the rhythms of their age. Their genius must be adapted, in a phrase from William James, "to the receptivities of the moment." Leaders are useless without followers. "There goes the mob," said the French politician, hearing a clamor in the streets. "I am their leader. I must follow them." Great leaders turn the inchoate emotions of the mob to purposes of their own. They seize on the opportunities of their time, the hopes, fears, frustrations, crises, potentialities. They succeed when events have prepared the way for them, when the community is awaiting to be aroused, when they can provide the clarifying and organizing ideas. Leadership completes the circuit between the individual and the mass and thereby alters history.

It may alter history for better or for worse. Leaders have been responsible for the most extravagant follies and most monstrous crimes that have beset suffering humanity. They have also been vital in such gains as humanity has made in individual freedom, religious and racial tolerance, social justice, and respect for human rights.

There is no sure way to tell in advance who is going to lead for good and who for evil. But a glance at the gallery of men and women in MODERN WORLD LEADERS suggests some useful tests.

One test is this: Do leaders lead by force or by persuasion? By command or by consent? Through most of history leadership was exercised by the divine right of authority. The duty of followers was to defer and to obey. "Theirs not to reason why/Theirs but to do and die." On occasion, as with the so-called enlightened despots of the eighteenth century in Europe, absolutist leadership was animated by humane purposes. More often, absolutism nourished the passion for domination, land, gold, and conquest and resulted in tyranny.

The great revolution of modern times has been the revolution of equality. "Perhaps no form of government," wrote the British historian James Bryce in his study of the United States, *The American Commonwealth,* "needs great leaders so much as democracy." The idea that all people should be equal in their legal condition has undermined the old structure of authority, hierarchy, and deference. The revolution of equality has had two contrary effects on the nature of leadership. For equality, as Alexis de Tocqueville pointed out in his great study *Democracy in America,* might mean equality in servitude as well as equality in freedom.

"I know of only two methods of establishing equality in the political world," Tocqueville wrote. "Rights must be given to every citizen, or none at all to anyone . . . save one, who is the master of all." There was no middle ground "between the sovereignty of all and the absolute power of one man." In his astonishing prediction of twentieth-century totalitarian dictatorship, Tocqueville explained how the revolution of equality could lead to the *Führerprinzip* and more terrible absolutism than the world had ever known.

But when rights are given to every citizen and the sovereignty of all is established, the problem of leadership takes a new form, becomes more exacting than ever before. It is easy to issue commands and enforce them by the rope and the stake, the concentration camp and the *gulag*. It is much harder to use argument and achievement to overcome opposition and win consent. The Founding Fathers of the United States understood the difficulty. They believed that history had given them the opportunity to decide, as Alexander Hamilton wrote in the first Federalist Paper, whether men are indeed capable of basing government on "reflection and choice, or whether they are forever destined to depend . . . on accident and force."

Government by reflection and choice called for a new style of leadership and a new quality of followership. It required leaders to be responsive to popular concerns, and it required followers to be active and informed participants in the process. Democracy does not eliminate emotion from politics; sometimes it fosters demagoguery; but it is confident that, as the greatest of democratic leaders put it, you cannot fool all of the people all of the time. It measures leadership by results and retires those who overreach or falter or fail.

It is true that in the long run despots are measured by results too. But they can postpone the day of judgment, sometimes indefinitely, and in the meantime they can do infinite harm. It is also true that democracy is no guarantee of virtue and intelligence in government, for the voice of the people is not necessarily the voice of God. But democracy, by assuring the right of opposition, offers built-in resistance to the evils inherent in absolutism. As the theologian Reinhold Niebuhr summed it up, "Man's capacity for justice makes democracy possible, but man's inclination to justice makes democracy necessary."

A second test for leadership is the end for which power is sought. When leaders have as their goal the supremacy of a master race or the promotion of totalitarian revolution or the acquisition and exploitation of colonies or the protection of greed and privilege or the preservation of personal power, it is likely that their leadership will do little to advance the cause of humanity. When their goal is the abolition of slavery, the liberation of women, the enlargement of opportunity for the poor and powerless, the extension of equal rights to racial minorities, the defense of the freedoms of expression and opposition, it is likely that their leadership will increase the sum of human liberty and welfare.

Leaders have done great harm to the world. They have also conferred great benefits. You will find both sorts in this series. Even "good" leaders must be regarded with a certain wariness. Leaders are not demigods; they put on their trousers one leg after another just like ordinary mortals. No leader is infallible, and every leader needs to be reminded of this at regular intervals. Irreverence irritates leaders but is their salvation. Unquestioning submission corrupts leaders and demeans followers. Making a cult of a leader is always a mistake. Fortunately hero worship generates its own antidote. "Every hero," said Emerson, "becomes a bore at last."

The single benefit the great leaders confer is to embolden the rest of us to live according to our own best selves, to be active, insistent, and resolute in affirming our own sense of things. For great leaders attest to the reality of human freedom against the supposed inevitabilities of history. And they attest to the wisdom and power that may lie within the most unlikely of us, which is why Abraham Lincoln remains the supreme example of great leadership. A great leader, said Emerson, exhibits new possibilities to all humanity. "We feed on genius. . . . Great men exist that there may be greater men."

Great leaders, in short, justify themselves by emancipating and empowering their followers. So humanity struggles to master its destiny, remembering with Alexis de Tocqueville: "It is true that around every man a fatal circle is traced beyond which he cannot pass; but within the wide verge of that circle he is powerful and free; as it is with man, so with communities." ●

The Presidency

ROH MOO HYUN, A FARM BOY FROM HUMBLE BEGINNINGS, BECAME president of the Republic of South Korea in December 2002. Elected to the country's highest position, Roh confronted a shadowed past of political and economic obsessives, catastrophic wars, and a global nuclear crisis.

South Korea was created when the Korean Peninsula was divided into two nations after World War II (1939–1945). A nation of mountain ranges and low-lying plains surrounded on the west and southwest coasts by over 3,500 small islands, it is roughly the size of the state of Indiana and is home to 50 million people. "In Korea both comedy and tragedy are extravagantly picturesque," wrote Burton Holmes in 1899 in *Burton Holmes Travelogues*. Indeed, the "Land of the Morning Calm" has long lingered in misty dreams and periods of violent reality.

Hours before Roh Moo Hyun's swearing in on February 25, 2003, North Korea test-fired a missile into the East Sea between

THE DIPLOMATIC NIGHTMARE WOULD UNNERVE EVEN A SEASONED STATESMAN, WHICH ROH WAS NOT.

Japan and the Korean Peninsula. The week before, *Time* magazine reported in its February 24, 2003 issue, "The North warned that it might abandon the 1953 Korean War armistice, and sent a MiG-19 jet fighter for a provocative two-minute swoop over South Korean airspace." If these daunting incidents were not enough to throw a new, untested leadership into a quagmire, the threat from North Korean dictator Kim Jong Il to arm himself with nuclear weapons and turn the peninsula into "smoking ashes" was.

Unlike South Korea, North Korea suffers from a hard-line Communist regime, a deteriorating economy, and severe food shortages. Its abundant mineral and hydroelectric resources have been used to develop its military strength and heavy industry. Relations with the United States declined after President George W. Bush included North Korea with Iraq and Iran in his January 31, 2002, speech as part of an "axis of evil." According to *Time*, "North Korea wants the U.S. to promise not to attack it and is demanding direct talks with the Bush administration. The U.S. says it wants multilateral talks and won't begin serious negotiations until the North dismantles its nuclear weapons program."

At this critical juncture in Korean history, Roh stepped into perhaps the most dangerous contest in the nation's long and fractured history. Hundreds of years of conflict with China, Japan, Manchuria, and Russia pales alongside a nuclear bomb explosion. The diplomatic nightmare would unnerve even a seasoned statesman, which Roh was not. Before attaining the presidency, he served in only two administrative positions. A foreign policy novice and political outsider, he was overwhelmingly voted into office by his straight talk and fearless independence, which appeared to fit the youthful national mood.

When he was elected to the presidency, Roh Moo Hyun *(right)* assured the South Korean public that he would continue the work of his predecessor, Kim Dae Jung *(left)* in establishing a diplomatic relationship with North Korea. Known as the "Sunshine Policy," the South Korean government agreed to send food and economic aid to North Korea in exchange for the eventual reunification of the two countries and the reunion of countless families separated by the border.

In his inaugural speech, Roh cast himself in the role of peacemaker and conceded that North Korea was actively pursuing a global nuclear threat. But he stressed a desire to keep open lines of communication and negotiate with North Korea rather than take military action, referring to the "Sunshine Policy" of his predecessor, Kim Dae Jung. At an unprecedented summit in Pyongyang, North Korea, on June 13, 2000, President Kim Dae Jung and North Korean leader Kim Jong Il had agreed to work for reconciliation and eventual reunification of their two countries. For his efforts, Kim Dae Jung was named the winner of the 2000 Nobel Peace Prize.

CRITICISM FROM THE OPPOSITION

According to CNN.com's "Profile: President-elect Roh Moo Hyun," Roh's opponents were quick to attack his reconciliation forum and to brand him a "dangerous radical, ignorant of foreign policy and further noted his previous association that called for withdrawal of some 30,000 U.S. troops based in South Korea." Since the end of World War II and the division of North and South Korea, the United States has maintained a huge military presence in South Korea, which is unacceptable to many Koreans. In 1954, the United States and South Korea signed the ROK-U.S. Mutual Security Agreement, in which they agreed to defend each other in the event of outside aggression. The United States Armed Forces had the right to station troops in the Republic of Korea if it determined that such action would be a national security issue for the time being. Donald F. Gregg, president of the Korean Society and former U.S. ambassador to South Korea said, "For decades it was the threat from North Korea that was the glue that held the alliance together."

Showing newly polished statesmanship, Roh was quick to recognize this misstep. The following spring he told a visiting U.S. diplomat he had "grown more realistic" about the ROK-U.S. Alliance as it stands today, according to CNN.com's "Profile: President-elect Roh Moo Hyun."

In opposition to the idea of reunification of North and South Korea, some South Koreans warned that the country would be economically undesirable. They reasoned that thousands of poor and famished peasants, from a collapsing and impoverished economy, would cross the Demilitarized Zone (DMZ) and flood the south.

"Regardless of whatever causes North Korea embraces," Roh said seven months later, according to *NewsHour*, "the series of nuclear measures taken by North Korea is not desirable for peace and stability. It will never promote the stability and prosperity of North Korea itself. North Korea must withdraw its recent nuclear measures and restore the relevant facilities and equipment to their original state." Roh's other campaign issues included reforms to end labor conflicts and to bridge regional rivalries—hotly debated issues that run tangent to the nuclear question and affect the entire international community.

Roh had established three goals for his government: democracy for the people, a society of balanced development, and an era of peace and prosperity. He further directed that the "Sunshine Policy" maxim be changed to the "Peace and Prosperity Policy."

CORRUPTION AND SCANDAL

If President Roh's ambitious platform was stretched with human rights and democratic intentions, it also was plagued with calamity. The old corrupt ways of doing business appeared to throw a wrench into Roh's good-deed endeavors and Kim's Nobel Peace Prize.

A few months after Roh's inauguration, scandal rocked his administration when he was accused of accepting $9.7 million in illegal campaign contributions. Next, the administration was accused of "extortion payments" that were made to negotiate with North Korea. The administration was hounded by allegations that Hyundai Group—manufacturer of cars, trucks, buses, and ships, and one of South Korea's biggest conglomerates—funneled $500 million to North Korea to secure business deals and to smooth the way for the landmark June 2000 summit between then President Kim Dae Jung and Kim Jong Il. *Time* magazine reported that 70 percent of South Koreans wanted a full investigation of the scandal. Roh promised that "future aid payments will be made in the open instead of furtively."

Roh's five-year term certainly had incidents of abusive dealings. In March 2004, barely into his presidency, Roh was impeached for illegal electioneering and charges of incompetency. The government was forced into two months of political limbo. But, two months later, according to BBC News, the Constitutional Court overturned the charges and said "Roh had violated the law, but not gravely enough to warrant his removal from office."

Roh has said the person he respects the most is Abraham Lincoln. The sixteenth U.S. president prevailed in giving hope and courage to countless people. Lincoln came from a humble family background, like Roh, and became a great leader because he refused to abuse the mighty presidential power even in times of adversity. "Lincoln was also president during very trying times," said Roh when asked why he compared himself to Lincoln. "Yet he built up a very strong country."

Sealed tight in the 1600s after being invaded and conquered so many times, Korea closed its borders to all nations except China. Isolated from the developing world, the country became known as the Hermit Kingdom, which lasted until the early twentieth century. Eventually, world treaties were negotiated with Korea, and its border restrictions were relaxed. Once more, neighboring lands declared war on Korean soil, and foreign powers split the nation in two and ruled it largely by foreign authoritarian regimes. South Korea still endures many difficulties: foreign exploitation, interior struggles, and now the threat of nuclear annihilation from its northern half.

Despite his initial popularity, Roh was almost ejected from office shortly after he took the presidency. Accusing him of breaking a minor election law, his enemies started an impeachment process that stalled government proceedings for two months as South Korea waited to see what would happen to its leader.

Would a new generation of politicians be able to fulfill Korea's democratic concepts and actively participate in world affairs? Would President Roh make good on his campaign promises?

TWO PRESIDENTS IN THAILAND

In October 2003, President Roh met with President George W. Bush in Bangkok, Thailand. He would meet with the U.S. president six times. This time, they discussed ways to make sure trade between the United States and South Korea was free and fair, and that the Korean Peninsula was free of nuclear weapons. Roh commended the United States's efforts in bringing peace and democracy to Iraq and its reconstruction of Iraq's economy. He asked President Bush two questions: How could South Korea cooperate in regard to Iraq? And what were the goals of APEC (Asian-Pacific Economic Cooperation, founded in 1989), a forum to further trade and investment between the nations and the rest of the world?

Bush replied, "We want the world to be more free and peaceful. . . . I'm so grateful for South Korea's support in places like Iraq."

The following February, the South Korean parliament approved a plan for deployment of 3,000 troops to Iraq. Marines, Special Forces commandos, military engineers, and medics were added to a strong combat force of 465 Korean military medics and engineers who had been in Iraq since May 2003. The additional forces were responsible for security and reconstruction in Kirkuk, Iraq.

FUTURE ISSUES FOR SERIOUS STUDY

In November 2004, APEC's leaders acted to increase global trade. APEC planned to promote policies to spur the economic growth of the area and to fight actions to reduce piracy and trade in counterfeit goods. Reports of copyright infringements and unfair labor practices of U.S.-imported items such as popular designer garments, inexpensive clothing, and high-tech digital products continued to draw critical attention. Also under discussion was the Korea-U.S. Free Trade Agreement (FTA). The stakes were high for the two countries, reported *Korea Policy Review* in April 2007. "The U.S. has an $11 million deficit in auto trade with Korea, which is 82 percent of the total deficit between the two countries," added Stephen Collins, president of the U.S. Automotive Trade Policy Council. "In simple numbers auto trade between the U.S. and Korea is so lopsided that it cannot be seriously justified by any credible economic or market-based rationales." Economic and security issues between the United States and South Korea are as contentious as the North Korean nuclear issue.

Perhaps temporarily shadowed by reunification was President's Roh stand on constitutional revisions. It was centered on a four-year presidential term with the possibility of being reelected to a second term, and it also revised terms for members of the National Assembly. According to the draft presented March 8, 2007, as stated in the *Korean Policy Review*, Roh's proposal cited "aims at reinforcing accountability, continuity, stability, and efficiency in governing the nation and building a new pillar supporting national development in the 21st century."

There is no doubt President Roh walked a political tightrope. His undertakings appeared far-ranging, controversial, and sometimes ingratiating, yet they were seemingly aimed at the betterment of South Korea. His leadership was paramount to successful participation in world affairs, safety from nuclear destruction, and the nation's economic and democratic stability.

Roh is said to have been an atypical Korean president in that he was not authoritarian like his many predecessors. He is a humble person, tending to be shy, and kind and approachable; many people have called him a "grassroots president." However, Roh was entrenched in a nation conflicted with varying ideological points of view and a catastrophic threat of nuclear destruction.

A study of old Korea, Roh Moo Hyun's past, and his political legacy will provide readers with a clearer understanding of South Korea and its dynamic position in the international community.

2

Shadows of Korea's Past

AFTER BECOMING PRESIDENT OF SOUTH KOREA, ROH MOO HYUN SPOKE numerous times of the tumultuous mistakes of a failed history. At a Memorial Day celebration in 2006 he urged, "Never again should we repeat such a tragic history that demands the sacrifice of our people. We should never allow for the reoccurrence of the same suffering by neglecting to learn from the history of our compatriots who sacrificed themselves, or by not putting into practice what we learned."

KOREA MARKS 5,000 YEARS OF HISTORY

Archaeologists have found evidence that people settled on the rugged Korean Peninsula nearly 30,000 years ago. They probably came from regions to the north and northwest—Siberia, Manchuria, and Mongolia—to hunt and fish in the heavily forested mountains and deep harbors. Yet, little else is known of prehistoric times until 2333 B.C., when the first Korean state developed along the Taedong River, near present-day Pyongyang. From that day, Koreans mark 5,000 years of history. The city was called Old Choson ("Land of the Morning Calm"). Today South Koreans refer to it as *Han'guk.*

According to a Koryŏ legend, the ancient king, Tan'gun, founded the land and built his palace near Pyongyang. The text gave this version of his birth:

> Long ago there lived a she-bear and a tigress in the same cave. They prayed to Hwanung (the king who descended from heaven) to be blessed with incarnation as human beings. The king took pity on them and gave each a bunch of mugwort and twenty pieces of garlic: "If you eat this holy food and do not see the sunlight for one hundred days, you will become human beings."
>
> The she-bear and the tigress ate the garlic and retired in the cave. In twenty-one days the bear, who had faithfully observed the king's instructions, became a woman. But the tigress, who had disobeyed, remained in her original form.
>
> The bear woman could find no husband, so she prayed under a sandalwood tree to be blessed with a child. Hwanung heard her plea and married her. She conceived a son who was called Tan'gun Wanggom, the King of Sandalwood.

In November 1993, the Korean Central News Agency reported, "The founding of Old Choson by Tan'gun . . . marked an epochal occasion in the formation of the Korean nation. With the founding of the state of Kojson (Old Choson) an integrated political unit was established, blood ties and cultural commonness of the population were strengthened, and their political and economic ties became closer, which gave momentum to the formation of the nation. . . . The Koreans are a homogenous nation who inherited the same blood and culture consistently down through history."

Tan'gun's kingdom lasted a thousand years. In 1429, the people built a temple in Pyongyang to honor the long-ago king of Sandalwood. The ancient shrine stood until the Korean War, when it was blown up. The traditional founding of Korea by Tan'gun is celebrated on October 3, National Foundation Day.

STRONG CHINESE INFLUENCE

China, to the west across the Yellow Sea and bordering on the north, greatly influenced Korean civilization. As far back as 108 B.C., the Han dynasty established four territories in the northern half of the Korean Peninsula. Developments coincided with the emergence of the iron culture—the molding of agricultural implements such as hoes, sickles, and plowshares.

In 75 B.C., Korea regained control of three of the territories; the fourth, Lalang, remained under Chinese control. For the next four centuries, Lalang was a great center of Sino-Korean statecraft, art, iron culture, and commerce. Monks were dispatched to China to learn practical innovations such as systems of government and writing. By the first century B.C., three kingdoms had been established: Silla in 57 B.C., Goguryeo in 37 B.C., and Baekje in 18 B.C. In 1913, renowned Japanese archaeologist Sekino Tadashi unearthed extraordinary relics from this period. Sixty years later, other archaeologists discovered a burial chamber called the Heavenly Horse Tomb. The anonymous grave was a gravel mound with a double wooden coffin beneath, typical of a Silla burial. Excavations revealed a gold crown and a mural painted on birch bark showing a white horse flying to heaven.

In A.D. 313, Korean forces drove the Chinese out and took control of the northern half of the country. Buddhism, which the Koreans learned from the Chinese, became the chief religion of the three kingdoms. In the fourth and fifth centuries, reservoirs for irrigation were constructed and rice agriculture developed in the rich alluvial valleys and plains. For the next 200 years, war raged among the three kingdoms. With help

The Silla kingdom of Korea was one of the world's most advanced early civilizations. Along with an observatory, Silla's contributions to architecture and art helped shape modern-day Korean culture. Remnants of the structures and monuments erected during this time period still can be seen in Kyongju, South Korea *(above)*.

from the Chinese Tang dynasty, the kingdom of Silla finally conquered the remaining two regions and gained control of most of the peninsula.

SILLA'S CULTURAL SPHERE

Silla once was called The City of Gold. Its advanced civilization excelled in art, music, and literature. Astronomy, calendrical science, and mathematics were developed, and magnificent monuments were erected. Extravagance flourished. One of the oldest observatories in Asia, it was popularized by Queen Seondeok. It is said she sat long hours in the Tower of Moon and Stars contemplating the heavens. The observatory stands on a platform of 12 rectangular stones; 365 granite blocks are stacked in 30 layers that taper toward the top to give stability. Because of the number of blocks, 365, historians suggest the number matches the days of a year.

A voluntary military organization called the Flower of Youth Corps trained students in the art of war, literature, and community life. They were directed to observe loyalty to the monarch and filial piety to parents, and to be amicable to friends. Never were they to retreat in battle, yet they had an aversion to unnecessary killing.

The construction of Hwangnyongsa Temple began in 553. Silla's six largest Buddha statues were erected in 574. Seventy-five years later, master architect Abiji of the kingdom of Baekje built a nine-story wooden pagoda. Tragically, the temple was destroyed by the Mongol invasion of 1238. But the existing site reveals the temple layout with its seven courts. To the northeast is the ancient Imhaejeon Palace and Anapji, the "Pond for Geese and Ducks" designed in the shape of Silla. It was built by the thirtieth ruler of Silla, Munmu.

CONFUCIANISM'S INFLUENCE

The Chinese introduced Confucianism, which became a strong influence on Korean thought, behavior, and education. The Mandate of Heaven, a traditional Chinese concept similar to the European code of Divine Right, legitimized rule but allowed the ouster of unjust rulers. In Chinese thought, a successful revolt was considered evidence that the Mandate of Heaven had passed; it was wrong to revolt, but a successful insurrection was understood as evidence of divine approval.

An infamous allegiance, the Warrior Oath, symbolized the mix of Buddhism and Confucianism and characterized contemplation. In the early seventh century, warriors were required to honor its five injunctions: loyalty to the king, filial love toward one's parents, fidelity in friendship, bravery in battle, and chivalry in warfare.

From the seventh century until the twentieth century, Korea existed as a single independent country. The future president Roh Moo Hyun and his parents and grandparents were predominately from Korea's agricultural society. Families of several generations lived harmoniously in small villages and farmed rice and grain. Customarily, the oldest male served as head of the household, and all members were expected to obey their elders without question.

Battered by elitists, politicians, and rebelling peasants, the kingdom of Silla slowly broke apart. It was reunited in 918 by General Wang Kon, who extended its northern border to the mouth of the Yalu River and renamed the country Goryeo, or Koryŏ, a shortened form of Goguryeo, or Koguryŏ. The name "Korea" comes from Koryŏ. The government built schools and encouraged the development of printing; 80,000 woodblocks were produced for teaching instruction. In 1234, the Koreans invented the world's first movable metal printing type.

MONGOLS INVADE KOREA

Fidelity and social life drastically changed with the Mongol invasion. Commanded by Kublai Khan, grandson of the great Genghis Khan, Koreans were forced to participate in two failed attempts to invade Japan. Peasants and farmers lost their land to Korean aristocrats, and artisans became slaves, some given in tribute to the Mongols. With the rise of the Chinese Ming dynasty, one hundred years later, Korea regained its prominence but split apart. One side allied with the Mongols, the other with the Ming dynasty. Both fought for control of the peninsula. In 1388, General Yi Sŏng-gye led the Ming forces to victory. But the Mongol rampage had left the land and its people in shambles.

General Yi declared himself king of Korea and founded the Choson dynasty (also known as the Yi dynasty). He moved the capital to Seoul and constructed a 10.5-mile (16.89-kilometer) wall around the city. He promoted arts and literature and placed all Korean land under his control, doling it out to his favorite military leaders and government officials. Confucianism replaced Buddhism as the state religion. In 1443, scholars created the Korean alphabet. The Choson dynasty lasted until 1910. Yi's grandson, King Sejong, is regarded as Korea's greatest ruler. North Koreans use the name Choson for their country.

In 1592, Japan successfully invaded Korea and conquered Busan, Seoul, and Pyongyang. Six years later, with the help of China, the Koreans drove the Japanese out. Historians give victory credit to Admiral Yi Sunsin, inventor of the first armored warship, called a turtle boat. With iron plates on its top and a large sail similar to that of a Chinese junk, a dozen sailors pulled its oars. Cannons shot thunder bombs of gunpowder and iron splinters. A fearsome dragon was mounted on the ship's head. Built to Yi's specifications, the ship was 65 feet (19.8 meters) long and 15 feet (4.5 m) amidships, and its sides were 8 feet (2.4 m) high. Thick wooden boards and long iron spikes protected its shell back. Humiliated by defeat, Japanese forces withdrew, taking 10,000 ears of dead Korean and Chinese soldiers. The ears (used for body count) were buried in Kyoto. In 1994, the ears were unearthed and returned to Korea. The Yi dynasty surrendered to the northern invading enemy in 1630, but its rulers remained as feudal lords, paying tribute.

HERMIT KINGDOM

Invaded, conquered, and repressed so many times, in 1642 Korea sealed its borders to all nations except China and built a high wooden palisade fence across its northern border. Isolated from the developing world, the country became known as the Hermit Kingdom. Westerners applied the label as a racist symbol for the people. The term often is used by Koreans themselves to describe premodern Korea. The first documented use of the term "hermit" was the title of William Elliot Griffis's 1882 book, *Corea: The Hermit Nation.* Griffis never visited Korea, did not speak the language, and had no firsthand experience with the country. He supported the invasion and occupation of Korea by Japan, and his writings attempted to prove the superiority of Japan. The book circulated in North America, led to tacit approval of Japan's incursions into Korea, and justified Japan's actions, which showed the Korean people to be primitive, uncultured, unable to function internationally, and needing Japanese direction.

During this dark era, Roman Catholic missionaries arrived from China with delicate wares and new inventions like alarm clocks and telescopes. Unwelcome, the missionaries were persecuted and thousands of Koreans who practiced the religion were killed. Around 1830, European Catholics and Protestant missionaries introduced social and democratic concepts of individualism, equality of women, and national self-determination.

COMPLICATIONS OF FOREIGN INTERVENTION

Japan was the first to penetrate Korea's isolation in 1897. Japan forced an unequal treaty giving Japanese nationals extraterritorial rights. Japan opened three ports to trade: Busan, Inchon, and Wonsan. The United States, China, Russia, and Britain next signed trade and diplomatic agreements. Forced by the new invaders, the Korean court split into pro-Chinese, pro-Japanese, and pro-Russian factions. Rebellion followed.

According to *Foreign Area Studies from the American University*, the Japanese minister of Korea, unable to quell internal dissentions, masterminded the assassination of the Korean queen. Incensed, the king turned for help to Japan's adversary, Russia.

In 1894, fired up by religious fervor and a corrupt and oppressive regime, ninety-five rebels from the Eastern Learning Movement staged a revolt. Unable to quell a spreading rebellion, the Korean court asked China to send troops. Japan countered with its own army. Rather than crush the disobedience, conflict arose between the two opposing countries and resulted in the Sino-Japanese War (1894–1895).

Victorious, Japan established rule over Korea and dictated measures to prevent further violence. Under the Treaty of Shimonoseki, Japan secured "independence" of Korea and cession of Taiwan, the nearby Pescadores Islands, and the Liaodong Peninsula for a naval base. A secret Sino-Russian treaty signed one year later granted Russia the right to build and operate the Chinese Eastern Railway across northern Manchuria, as well as acquisitions of Korea's forests and mines.

Pressured by the European countries, Japan returned the Russian-occupied peninsula and established Port Arthur. But rivalry between Japan and Russia over control ignited the Russo-Japanese War of 1904–1905, which was won by Japan. Thereafter, according to author Bruce Cumings in *Korea's Place in the Sun*, Russia acknowledged Japan's "paramount political, military, and economic interests in Korea." Two months later, Japan annexed Korea. Russia nevertheless gained considerable influence in the rise of Korea's Communist politics.

Korea's next 50 years were cemented by horrific tragedy and acute foreign exploitation. Across the East Sea, the rising imperial Japanese nation became the first country to subdue Russia, one of the "great powers," wrote Bruce Cumings.

The Treaty of Portsmouth, ending the Russo-Japanese War, was signed September 5, 1905. Russia recognized Japan's paramount rights in Korea. The treaty was brokered by America's twenty-sixth president, Theodore Roosevelt, at Portsmouth, New Hampshire. One year later, President Roosevelt received the Nobel Peace Prize for his part in the negotiations.

After the Japanese invaded Korean territory in the Sino-Japanese War *(above)*, they forced the "Hermit Kingdom" to open itself up to trade—but the benefits would go mostly to Japan. Foreign influence flooded government proceedings as the members of the Korean court began to ally themselves with one of several international powers in their midst.

THE TAFT-KATSURA AGREEMENT

Two months before the Treaty of Portsmouth was signed, another conference took place between the United States and Japan with an agreement that sealed the significance of Portsmouth. In a trade-off known as the Taft-Katsura Agreement, Japan agreed not to question American rights in

Hawaii or in its Philippines colony. In exchange, the United States would not challenge Japan's expansion on the Korean Peninsula. These secret documents, and Roosevelt's confirming telegram, were found in the archives of the office of the Ministry of Foreign Affairs. A copy resides in the Washington University Far East Library.

On July 27, 1905, Secretary of War William Howard Taft met with Japan's Count Katsura to resolve grievances between the two countries. "Taft observed that Japan's only interest in the Philippines would be, in his opinion, to have those islands governed by a strong and friendly nation like the United States. . . . Count Katsura agreed that Korea being the direct cause of our war with Russia, it is a matter of absolute importance to Japan that a complete solution of the peninsula question should be made as a logical consequence of the war. If left to herself after the war, Korea will certainly draw back to her habit of improvidently entering into any agreements or treaties with other powers, thus resuscitating the same international complications as existed before the war. . . . Japan feels absolutely constrained to take some definite step with a view to precluding the possibility of Korea falling into her former condition and of placing us again under the necessity of entering upon another foreign war. Secretary Taft fully admitted the justness of the Count's observations and remarked to the effect that, in his personal opinion, the establishment by Japanese troops of a suzerainty [a state that exercises control over another state; an overlord] over Korea to the extent of requiring Korea to enter into no foreign treaties without the consent of Japan was a logical result of the present war and would directly contribute to permanent peace in the East. His judgment was that President Roosevelt would concur . . . although he had no authority to give assurance. . . ."

In a telegram dated July 31, 1905, President Roosevelt concurred: "Your conversation with Count Katsura absolutely

KOREA NOW NO LONGER
EXISTED AS A NATION.

correct in every respect. Wish you would state to Katsura that I confirm every word you have said."

Akira Iriye, author of *Pacific Estrangement: Japanese and American Expansion, 1897–1911*, wrote, "Japan had a 'free hand' in Korea after 1905, as the diplomatic historians say, because of its victories over China and Russia, and because of British and American support (the Anglo-Japanese Alliance concluded in 1902). As long as the direction of Japanese imperialism was directed toward Korea and Manchuria, which pushed it away from the Philippines or the many British colonies, it had the blessings of London and Washington."

Once again foreign intrusion dictated Korea's sovereignty.

JAPAN OCCUPIES KOREA

Korea now no longer existed as a nation. To supply its own country with chemicals, iron, and steel, Japan built heavy industries in Korea. Fertile farmlands were confiscated. Young Korean men were forcibly moved from the forested rolling hills and green plains to labor in cities, or they were shipped to Japan's South Pacific Islands. Two hundred thousand Korean men worked in Japanese coal mines. Groups of men dug an underground bunker beneath Mount Fuji for the safety of the imperial household. School children bowed to pictures of the emperor. Everyone participated in Japanese religious rituals. The Korean language was banned and replaced with Japanese. Anguished Koreans, acutely aware of the need to preserve their cultural identity, were forced to take Japanese-style names or face execution. During World War II, when threatened with death or imprisonment, many Koreans aided the Japanese war effort against the United States. Men were drafted into the Japanese military. Korean construction workers were sent to Hiroshima and Nagasaki, and 10,000 were killed in the catastrophic U.S. atomic bombing. Between 100,000 and 200,000 girls and women were forced into slavery as "comfort women" for the Japanese armed forces. Not until the 1990s did these women speak of the humiliation. But Japan continues to deny the allegations. The *Los Angeles Times*, on March 7, 2007, quoted Japanese prime minister Shinzo Abe as saying, "There is insufficient evidence to indicate Japan's official involvement in recruiting comfort women."

Japan has relentlessly voiced opposition to the Korean claims. "On the positive side the Japanese built schools, factories, and railroads; introduced many innovations in agriculture and fishery; and established modern, if not exactly democratic, legal and administrative systems . . . patterned on continental European models. These changes . . . benefited only a small minority of Japanese expatriates, Korean landowners, and entrepreneurs who were allowed to operate in the shadow of Japanese domination," reported the Foreign Area Studies of American University.

In December 1943, during World War II, President Franklin D. Roosevelt, Prime Minister Winston D. Churchill of Great Britain, and Generalissimo Chiang Kai-shek of China met at the Cairo Conference. They agreed that, as a result of Japan's expansion drive, it would be stripped of all its territories acquired since 1894. Korea had been one of the first. The three powers further agreed that, after the Allied victory, "in due course" Korea would be allowed to become free. In February 1945, at the Yalta Conference, the Soviet Union agreed on the same principle in its declaration of war against Japan. President Roosevelt and Marshal Joseph Stalin decided to establish an international trusteeship for Korea. But no decision was made on the exact procedure for governing the nation in the aftermath of victory.

CHAPTER

3

Division of North and South Korea

THE UNITED STATES DEFEATED JAPAN ON AUGUST 14, 1945; FORMAL surrender was September 2, 1945. Korea appeared to be free of hundreds of years of dictatorial regimes. It was not to be. At midnight four days before, on August 10–11, John J. McCloy of the State-War-Navy Coordinating Committee directed two young colonels, Dean Rusk and Charles H. Bonesteel, to find a place to divide Korea. The decision was hasty and unilateral. Given thirty minutes to do so, Rusk and Bonesteel looked at a map and chose the 38th parallel line because "it would place the capital city in the American zone," according to Foreign Relations of the United States (FRUS), 1945–1950, Vol. 6. The Soviets made no objections and the United States consulted none of its other allies.

On a warm summer day in August 1945, Russian soldiers marched into Korea. Twenty-nine days later, on September 8, the United States sent in its troops. In the north, the Soviet military

In 1948, two separate governments, South Korea and North Korea, were officially divided by the 38th parallel of latitude.

rapidly and efficiently organized Socialists and Communists. Although the two major powers, the United States and the Soviet Union, made efforts to allow Koreans to unite, their efforts for reunification failed. The United States submitted the problem to the newly formed United Nations (chartered by 50 nations on June 26, 1945). At this critical junction in Korea's tormented history, Roh Moo Hyun was born. Unbeknown to his parents, and to Roh, his life became significantly embedded in the perpetual chaos of South Korea.

Discussions among the two major powers and the UN lagged for two years as the Soviet Union refused to allow UN representatives to supervise an election to the newly formed Korean National Assembly. In 1948, two separate governments, South Korea and North Korea, were officially divided by the 38th parallel of latitude. In 1945 at the Yalta Conference, Great Britain, the United States, and the Soviet Union had agreed that if the Soviet Union assisted in defeating Japan, it would gain control of the northern part of the Korean Peninsula.

The Republic of Korea (ROK) was designated in the southern half with Seoul as its capital. The South Korean National Assembly elected Syngman Rhee president. A Communist-style government, the Democratic People's Republic of Korea (DPRK), assumed control of the North. Kim Il Sung, who headed the Workers' Party, became the leader of North Korea. With no give and take or mutual trust, both governments continued to represent all of Korea.

Roger Baldwin, former head of the American Civil Liberties Union, toured South Korea in 1947. In Bruce Cumings's book-*Korea's Place in the Sun*, Baldwin observed, "The country is literally in the grip of a police regime and a private terror. You get the general impression of a beaten, discouraged people . . . who want all foreigners to get out and let them build their nation." Yet according to Cumings's book, Baldwin thought that if America were to pull out, a civil war would result. After an American G-2 (intelligence) chief showed him political reports on the countryside, Baldwin then concluded that "a state of undeclared war" already existed in Korea. Yo Un-hyong (known to Americans as Lyuh Woon-hyung), key organizer of the Korean People's Republic in Seoul, added that the government was "full of Quislings" and "toadiers to the Americans," and that it was the American retention of the colonial police that was the key to the "present chaos."

YOUTH AND DETERMINATION

Roh Moo Hyun was born September 1, 1946, in the mountainous village of Bonghwa, in Gimhae city, Gyeongsang province, in the southeastern part of Korea. He was raised by his parents, Roh Pan-seok and Lee Sun-lye, in a thatched-roof house similar to that of other peach and chicken farmers, with two older brothers and two older sisters. "His family was poor but loving, and Roh was especially loved by everyone in the household probably because he was smart," noted the Seoul office of President Roh Moo Hyun. While he was growing up, his favorite school subjects were Korean language and history. He was—and still is—an avid reader, suggesting that one of his favorite books is the classic *Les Miserables* by Victor Hugo. In middle school he learned English and focused mainly on grammar and reading skills.

Years later, after Roh's ambitious venture into Korean politics, trifling stories of his youth began to circulate in international newspapers and magazines and on television. When Roh was a sixth grader at Daechang primary school, his family was unable to pay the school tuition. Stories went as follows: Roh's family's financial situation made him feel uncomfortable at school and sometimes made him feel small. But he had the support of his teacher, who encouraged him to run for president of the student council. At first Roh said he did not have the courage and resisted running, which disappointed her. In his elementary school records, reporters quoted a teacher saying Roh had "talents in all subjects, especially presentation of his opinions." Rather than let his teacher down, he entered the race. His campaign speech, outlining his ambition and future plans, impressed the teacher and his fellow students. He won easily with 302 votes out of 502 cast. Winning gave Roh self-assurance, and after becoming president of the Republic of Korea, he frequently spoke about the importance of self-assurance and visions for the future.

Time magazine reported on March 2, 2003, "Because of his stature [he was tiny but tough], classmates nicknamed him 'stone bean.' One day while trekking through soggy rice paddies to school an older boy, much bigger, pushed him around and called him names. Roh decided enough was enough and enlisted two friends to settle the score. When the bully taunted him again, the boys yelled, knocked him to the ground, and kicked him. The tyrant never bothered Roh again." Another story recounted that Roh was known as "a smart kid with a sharp tongue, a stubborn streak and a fondness for boozy boisterousness." In his autobiography, Roh freely admits that he was a hot-and-cold student in high school, doing well when he studied but suffering plummeting grades after he skipped class to smoke and drink with friends. Had the future human rights lawyer and South Korean president already demonstrated qualities of leadership, tenacity, truth, and world newsworthiness?

Rowdy behavior did not keep Roh from actively working hard. Unable to afford college, Roh was told by his eldest brother to enter the prestigious Bosan Commercial High School. At that time, highly qualified students were able to receive full scholarships, and upon graduation most landed stable jobs. After completing the three-year course, Roh worked at a small company making fishing nets. He soon knew he wanted more challenges and returned home. On his own he began to study for the national bar exam. Passing the bar meant he could become a judge, prosecutor, or lawyer. In order to buy books for the exam, he worked as a day laborer on construction sites. Once while working, he sustained severe injuries that left three of his teeth broken and his lips cut.

In 1973, Roh married his high-school sweetheart, Kwon Yang-suk; he often refers to her warm personality and diligence. They had two children, son Roh Geon-ho, born in 1973, and daughter Roh Jeong-yeon, born in 1975. Unable to continue his studies because of financial responsibilities to his young family, Roh enlisted in the army. After completing the three-year compulsory military service, he set his goals high and prepared for the law test. In 1975, after his third try, the self-taught young man passed South Korea's notoriously difficult bar exam. In a nation consumed with higher education, Roh earned a prestigious law degree despite a lack of financial support.

Recalling those difficult years, Roh wrote in *Common Sense or Hope*, "Every time I look back on my life, I am suddenly engulfed in a certain feeling. It is kind of a shame. It is exceptional, in a society which puts so much stress on one's educational background, that a man with only a vocational high school diploma was elected president," according to the official Web site of the South Korean government.

Roh has written four books. In his 1994 autobiography, *Honey, Please Help Me*, he renounced the wild habits of his youth, his hard drinking, and physically abusing his wife, Kwon Yang-suk. He credited his behavioral turnaround to reading a book about women's rights.

A LOOK BACK—THE KOREAN WAR

In 1948, the Soviets announced the withdrawal of all their troops in North Korea. Two separate political regimes were formally established, and two rival Korean governments with vastly different ideologies were soon in operation. A year later, the United States withdrew its troops. On June 25, 1950, the Communists launched a surprise attack on South Korea with an army of 60,000 troops. China and the Soviet Union had armed and staged the devastating offense that initiated the Korean War. Two days later, President Harry S. Truman ordered United States Air Force and Navy personnel to South Korea. The United Nations Security Council sent troops to join soldiers of the Republic of Korea (ROK).

In November 1950, UN troops reached the Chinese border only to be driven back by 200,000 Chinese who had crossed the Yalu River. All through the winter of 1951, Korean and American ground troops suffered biting winds and freezing cold. During the spring thaw, battle lines finally were stabilized near the original 38th parallel. Cease-fire talks began in July. Up against superior forces of Chinese and North Koreans, the South Koreans faced heavy fighting and great loss of life for two more years. An armistice finally was signed on July 27, 1953. The Demilitarized Zone was determined at the cease-fire and officially split the two countries along the 38th parallel. The DMZ is a strip of land roughly 2.5 miles (4 km) wide that runs for 155 miles (250 km), bisecting the peninsula. White markers along the length of the strip post signs to indicate the physical dividing line known as the Military Demarcation Line (MDL). A barbed-wire fence guards the outposts, and thousands of military personnel are stationed alongside the MDL. U.S. troops remain in South Korea.

Both sides suffered tremendous casualties. Thirty-four thousand American soldiers were killed and more than 100,000 were wounded. Approximately 500,000 Korean civilians and military personnel were killed. Hundreds of thousands of people were wounded, and cities and land were devastated. A permanent peace treaty has never been signed. Like thousands of other Koreans, Roh's life and that of his family were deeply affected by the war and the hardships that followed.

During the summer of 1950, when Communist Korean soldiers invaded the South, U.S. and UN troops assisted in launching an offensive on the Korean peninsula *(above)*. With the help of Chinese and Soviet forces, the Communists managed to hold on to territory and to draw a border between themselves and South Korea. This division would drastically change the lives of thousands of people.

AFTERMATH OF WAR

The war's end had left indelible marks on all of Korea. The entire peninsula was reduced to rubble. Fighting had wiped out farm crops. Food was scarce. Thousands of homes and many factories were destroyed. There was little industry and few electric power plants. As a result, employment was low, with unrest among the population. Hostilities between the Communist and non-Communist camps intensified, turning Koreans against Koreans. In North Korea, a large number of Chinese troops remained and began to play a prominent role in the new government. The United States military remained with some 30 bases, providing massive economic aid; the average inflow from 1953 to 1958 was U.S. $270 million a year, as reported by the Foreign Area Studies of American University. With so much money coming in, there was widespread fraud and corruption.

INTERNAL CONFLICT WITH SYNGMAN RHEE

The Korean National Assembly became increasingly critical of President Syngman Rhee's authoritarian rule and injustice. As beneficiary of billions of dollars of U.S. aid, Korea experienced widespread cases of fraud and government corruption: the tungsten dollar scandal of 1952, the raw cotton import case of 1954, and many other scams. "Rhee knew the United States had no one else to rely on but him. . . . That it happened to be American taxpayers' money was the least of his worries," wrote Bruce Cumings in *Archaeology, Descent, Emergence: Japan in British American Hegemony, 1900–1950*.

In the southern farming village where Roh Moo Hyun was growing up, he saw people divided by hate and human suffering. Like 20 million other war-damaged Koreans, his parents struggled to feed and educate their children. Preserving a family way of life was extremely difficult. Hardship and pain became absorbed by the youth.

To the north, in the capital of Seoul, acutely aware of the National Assembly's mounting dissatisfaction with him, Rhee pushed through a constitutional amendment that turned the election over to the people. But opposition to his authoritarian government continued.

RHEE HAD EMBEZZLED $20 MILLION
IN GOVERNMENT FUNDS.

A symbol of the democratic opposition and an adversary of Rhee was 29-year-old Kim Dae Jung. A devout Catholic from Haui-do, Jeolla region, an island off the South Korean coast, Kim first entered politics in 1954. Without sufficient backing and despite his popular opposition to Rhee, Kim lost his run for the presidency. Rhee was easily reelected and had the Constitution amended to permit him to serve more than two terms. He ran again and won. But on university campuses, student protests were gathering a groundswell of support for a change.

In an effort to upstart Korean economic reform, in 1960 the government adopted a comprehensive seven-year economic development plan. Before it could be implemented, a student revolution brought down the government. In March, still attempting to pacify his constituents and opposition, Rhee ran for a fourth term. Yet fate seemed to be against democratic reform. Rhee's opponent suddenly died, and Rhee's party won again.

Corruption, scandal, and a dictatorial regime went uncontrolled as riots ensued. Triggered by the incident, a new wave of demonstrations against Rhee's government were marked with widespread violence and police brutality. In April, 125 student protesters were shot by police. Aware he was rapidly losing support, Rhee resigned. Then his deputy minister of finance, Kim Yong Kap, announced that Rhee had embezzled $20 million in government funds. Political survival had played a more important role in the country's leadership than its suffering economy and hungry people. Exiled in Hawaii, Rhee died there in 1962.

GENERAL PARK CHUNG HEE

Dr. Chang Myon assumed leadership of the new government. However, his presidency (from July 1960 to May 1961) was short-lived. Even though an internal security policy was estab-lished to open a more political system of government, students marched on the assembly, demanding punishment for miscre-ants of Rhee's regime. Chang was unable to maintain order, and in a bloodless coup, armed forces seized power. General Park Chung Hee emerged as chairman of the ruling junta. He called for national elections to restore the government and won the presidency two years later.

ENTER KIM DAE JUNG

The young rebel Kim Dae Jung continued to draw public sup-port and was elected to the National Assembly. But another military coup led by Park axed Kim's appointment. In sub-sequent elections in 1963 and 1967, Kim proved himself an eminent opposition leader. During Park's regime, two Korean divisions were sent to fight alongside U.S. forces in Vietnam. South Korea was richly rewarded by Washington with war purchases that helped the economy and political tolerance. In the 1960s, revenues from the Vietnam War were the largest single source of foreign-exchange earnings for South Korea. In 1971, Kim Dae Jung ran a close race with Park, command-ing an unwavering loyalty among supporters from the Jeolla region—upward of 95 percent of the popular vote—a record unmatched in South Korean politics. Under Park, the country's export-oriented economy began to prosper. In 1971, negotia-tions between North and South Korea provided the first hope for peaceful reunification. One year later, an agreement was reached for the establishment of a joint effort to work out plans. A 1972 referendum allowed Park to be reelected for an unlimited series of six-year terms. He won again in 1973 and 1978, until another scandal rocked the country.

PARK'S ATTEMPTS FOR REUNIFICATION

In 1972, Park sent his intelligence chief, Lee Hu Rak, to Pyongyang to meet with Kim Il Sung. The North Korean ruler,

President Dwight D. Eisenhower welcomes Syngman Rhee to the United States in July 1954. South Korea's first president was dedicated to the cause of an independent, united Korea. Elected in exile, Rhee returned to South Korea to find his country, and himself, threatened by Communist guerillas from the north. He successfully petitioned for help from the U.S. and the UN in defending democracy on the Korean peninsula, but later resigned from the presidency due to a series of political scandals.

who lived in complete luxury and owned at least five palaces, allowed only a few favorites to share his lavish lifestyle. Uninvited guests were forbidden to step foot on roads that led to his residences, and traffic was banned when he traveled. Thousands of monuments in his honor bore his name, and adults wore badges with his photo. Yet when Lee returned, he praised Kim: "Quite a guy, very strong, one-man rule." Two years later, an unsuccessful assassination attempt against Park fatally wounded his wife. The killer, who had been instructed by North Korea, ended North-South dialogue. Donald Gregg of *Time Asia* wrote on August 23, 1999, that "Park must be given credit for beginning the process."

Kim Dae Jung was kidnapped from a hotel in Tokyo during Park's presidency. His hands and feet were bound, and he was held in a small boat on the Sea of Japan, ready to be thrown overboard at the first signal. U.S. ambassador Phillip Habib immediately ordered his aides to find out where Kim was being held. The next morning he was told that South Korean agents had seized Kim. Habib demanded an explanation from Park. As a result of the U.S. intervention, Kim was returned safely to Seoul. Kim next was imprisoned for participation in an anti-government proclamation and was banned from politics. He was sentenced to five years in prison. In 1978, his sentence was reduced to house arrest.

During Park's long reign, the Korean economy rose on financial pages, but chaos between prodemocratic factions did not. Park declared martial law and used draconian power to suppress his opposition, such as with Kim. He curtailed freedom of speech and of the press. Koreans who opposed Park were jailed, and he was denounced as a dictator. At the same time, tensions between the United States and North Korea reached a breaking point when two U.S. officers were killed on a routine mission near the DMZ. Three days later, North Korea issued a statement of "regret." Withdrawal of U.S. forces was postponed until relations between North and South Korea improved.

In 1977, newly elected U.S. president Jimmy Carter cut the defense budget by $6 billion. One of his first acts was to order the unilateral removal of all nuclear weapons from South Korea and to cut back the number of U.S. ground troops within four to five years. Carter planned to remove all but 14,000 U.S. Air Force personnel and logistic specialists by 1982. A year later, after cutting only 3,600 troops, he abandoned the effort. Carter visited Seoul in 1979 and, according to reporters who accompanied him, became so angry after meeting with President Park that he nearly overruled the reversal of the troop withdrawal policy he had come to Seoul to announce, according to Bruce Cumings.

In October of the same year, President Park was assassinated by Kim Jae Kyu, head of South Korea's Central Intelligence Agency, ending his 18-year regime. In December, the Electoral College elected Prime Minister Choi Kyu Hah president of South Korea. Choi immediately instituted military rule. One year later, after a period of internal turmoil, Chun Doo Hwan was elected president.

THE GWANGJU MASSACRE

"The saga of Koreans' sacrifices for freedom and justice is as thrilling and inspiring as its economic wonders," wrote Ritu Raj Subedi in the *Rising Nepal* newspaper of May 7, 2002. The democratic uprising known as the Gwangju Massacre occurred May 18, 1980, in Gwangju in the southwest region of the country. In a tragic repetition of its dark history, South Korea witnessed the rise of yet another military dictatorship. Major General Chun Doo Hwan had seized power through a coup d'etat after the assassination of President Park. To consolidate his power and to quell mounting civil unrest, Chun, a career soldier who fought alongside U.S. forces in Vietnam, enforced martial law and organized paratroopers in Operation Brilliant Leave.

According to journalist Subedi, South Korean public opinion held the United States responsible for the massacre. "The

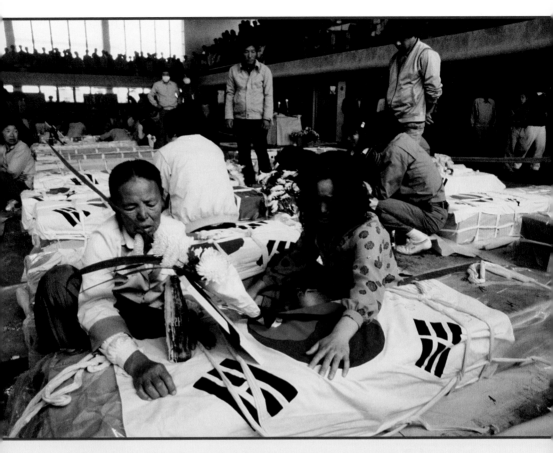

In the spring of 1980, a student-led demonstration in Gwangju, South Korea, was brutally crushed by the military. Filmed and aired on television, all of South Korea witnessed the tragic Gwangju Uprising of 1980 and mourned the deaths of the family members involved in the protests *(above)*.

historic event marked a major shift in the perception of many Koreans towards the United States. Until the Gwangju Massacre, Korea's elites, liberal political groups and a majority of populace had a strong faith that the U.S. was their true friend in their struggle for democracy. But when Washington backed the military juntas to trample the civilian revolt, their faith was shattered to the extent that some university graduates even committed suicide in an utter frustration."

On May 20, taxi drivers, with horns blaring and headlights glaring, roamed the city. Angry students set the Munhwa Broadcasting Company on fire, accusing broadcasters of distorting the news. On May 21, army troops fired indiscriminately into crowds demanding an apology from military authorities for beatings and arrests of pro-democracy fighters. A group calling themselves the Citizens Army formed a defensive force to fight the ROK army, and demonstrators lined up to donate blood for the wounded. Businesses provided free supplies to the protesters.

At Chonnam National University, students demonstrated against Chun and his failure to deliver promises of a new constitution and a specific timetable for free popular elections. They were beaten and chased off by paratroopers. Regrouping, the protesters began to march to the downtown area and were joined by middle-school and high-school students and sympathetic bystanders. The troops taunted the unruly crowd with fixed bayonets and tear gas. Arrests ensued. The citizens' council appealed to the American embassy to intervene. Three days later, after the U.S. aircraft carrier *Midway* had entered Korean waters, General John Wickham and his Twentieth Division of the ROK army patrolling the DMZ responded, according to a 1988 ROK National Assembly report.

At dawn on May 27, paratroopers and soldiers equipped with modern weapons and armored tanks advanced on demonstrators at the Provincial Hall. Shooting erupted. Caught on television, the ragtag Citizens Army fought back but was brutally crushed within one and a half hours. Nine days later, the Gwangju Democratic Uprising came to a bloody end. News spread rapidly throughout the international media. Chun arrested Kim Dae Jung for inciting the demonstrators and made himself president of the Fifth Republic. Afterward, a Citizens Resolution Committee formed to find a peaceful solution through negotiation. The military turned down the call.

According to the official data, the Gwangju Massacre left more than 154 people dead, 70 missing, and 3,028 wounded. Kim Dae Jung, the people's symbol of democratization, was found guilty and sentenced to death.

Anxious to mend relations between Seoul and the United States, President Ronald Reagan invited President Chun to Washington on the condition that he spare Kim's life. Kim's sentence was commuted to 20 years in prison. Chun purchased 36 American F-16 jet fighters, and about 4,000 U.S. troops were added to the existing troop commitment in Korea. Kim later was exiled to the United States, settling in Boston and teaching at Harvard University. In 1981, Reagan announced that no more U.S. troops would be withdrawn from South Korea.

At a Memorial Day celebration in 2006, President Roh Moo Hyun recalled the suffering brought on by self-interest, selfish desire, and a dogmatic ideology that did not tolerate difference. In a speech that easily could have been referring to the Gwangju Massacre, Roh said, "Despite liberation, the country was divided mainly because of the world order of East-West conflict, and consequently we had to suffer through a civil war. However, I am probably not the only one who thinks that if our people had come together as one, this great tragedy might have been avoided. Everyone shouted in one voice for national autonomy and unification. But by excluding each other and showing no toleration, we ended up killing each other—a dictatorship that used the pro-Japanese group that betrayed the nation, and ultimately brought about sacrifice," according to the Seoul office of the President of South Korea.

4

Roh Enters Korean Politics

AFTER EARNING HIS LAW DEGREE, ROH BECAME A TAX LAWYER. AMBITIOUS and determined to succeed, he passed the national examination for judges and became a regional judge in Daejon.

In 1978, he started a new career as a defense attorney and took what was to be a seminal case for his personal direction. He stated, "I was determined to address the irregular practice of taking kickbacks in the legal community," according to the Seoul office of the President of South Korea. Roh launched a career with a group of human rights lawyers to fight for civil rights and to advocate for labor rights and political dissidents. The decisive moment that led him into the democratization struggle came in 1981. Roh defended several student members of a book club who studied social science theories, including books on Socialism. The students were detained by the Chun government for possession of contraband literature. In an episode known as the Burim incident, the young men were held and tortured for almost two months. According to Roh, "The case was fabricated by the then-military-influenced authoritarian administration in order to stamp out political opponents." No longer able to bear the sight of the battered young students, he thundered into the courtroom blasting the cruel physical abuses and torture. His blistering rhetoric moved the courtroom audience to tears.

The Burim case fundamentally changed the course of Roh's life. According to the president's Seoul office, he has been quoted as saying, "When I saw a tortured student in the course of defending my client, a student involved in the Burim Incident, it occurred to me that it could also occur to my own children who would become college students sooner or later."

BLAME AND ACCUSATIONS

The Gwangju Massacre remained in the headlines, with high-level accusations and anti-American sentiment dominating. Dr. Sung Hae Kim, researcher at the Yonsei University, speaking with Ritu Raj Subedi in the *Rising Nepal* newspaper, wrote, "The U.S. and its military rulers thought the communist North was behind the Uprising and the U.S. supported the killing of innocent people. The massacre shattered their faith of the U.S. as an ally in the fight against military dictatorships."

Cho Hee Yeon, director of the Democracy and Social Movements Institute in Seoul countered, "Actually it was a civilian rebellion carried out without the support of Kim Il Sung. . . . The Gwangju Massacre sowed the seeds and millions of Koreans chanted, 'Yankee Go Home.'" During the continued criticism, the ROK–U.S. Alliance reached its lowest ebb, as did U.S. and Korean relations.

South Korea regarded the United States as its strongest and staunchest ally, and the United States valued South Korea as a key element in its strategic position in northeastern Asia. Since 1945, the United States had been Korea's single largest source of military and economic aid. But South Koreans were active protesters prepared to attack foreign intervention and local politicians on any occurrence.

THE 1980s

A new decade brought more social upheaval, the Olympic Games, and significant advances to Roh Moo Hyun's career. The South Korean constitution, introduced in 1948, was intended to foster an effective form of government, to ensure individual rights, to check corruption, and to safeguard against a dictatorial leadership. South Koreans—who for centuries were ruled by dictatorial governments that declared martial law on a whim, manipulated the constitution, and remained in power as long as they wished—were slow to assimilate to the new constitution. University students rallied and protested for a democratic government, but their vociferous intentions lacked sufficient support and went unheeded. Hard-line leadership continued, and human rights remained mute.

On October 27, 1980, the eighth revision of the 1948 constitutional document was adopted. This time the elected president held a single seven-year term and workers could form associations, engage in collective bargaining, and take collective action. Previous goals to enhance political legitimacy, military security, and economic development, and to maintain close ties with the United States did not change. The reforms shifted power to the National Assembly and "the dynamic export-oriented economy rose," as stated on washingtonpost.com.

Despite social unrest and an attempt on General Chun Doo Hwan's life, he was officially inaugurated president of the Republic of Korea the following February. The president's brother was arrested on corruption charges one month before the election. "That same year Chun purged thousands of government officials, some 37,000 journalists, students, teachers, labor organizers, and civil servants into 'purification camps,'" wrote Bruce Cumings.

South Koreans experienced a tumultuous year in 1983, with the attempted assassination of their president and his cabinet in Burma (now Myanmar) and the escalation of the Cold War. While the death of four ministers during the Burma incident was distressing for South Korea, the possibility of a U.S. nuclear strike on the Korean peninsula angered South Koreans. Both President Reagan *(left)* and President Chun Doo Hwan *(right, standing with Mrs. Reagan)* worked together to relieve the strain in relations between the two countries.

EFFORTS FOR REUNIFICATION

Ever since the peninsula was divided, there has been a strong belief among many South Koreans that the country should be reunited with the North. It is estimated that 10 million South and North Korean families have ties in North Korea. Numerous meetings have been held between Red Cross workers and family reunification projects. But whenever reunification efforts have seemed likely, grave incidents have occurred and have stalled any interaction.

In October 1983, a terrorist bomb in Rangoon, Burma (now the country of Myanmar), took out much of the traveling South Korean cabinet. President Chun narrowly escaped. A Burmese court determined that North Koreans were behind the bombing. As expected, further diplomatic relations between the North and South diminished.

That year, U.S. defense secretary Casper Weinberger declared Korea "a vital interest for the United States," and he proposed a five-year defense guidance. The document called for "horizontal escalation," which could mean that if the Soviets were to attack in the Persian Gulf, the United States might respond by attacking at a location of its own choosing. The document declared that Korea was such a location. The scenario so horrified Koreans that during President Ronald Reagan's term, South Koreans "shouted themselves hoarse in opposition to the U.S. policy," according to the *Korean Herald* of April 7, 1983.

In the meantime, Roh was serving as director of the Research Center for Environment Pollution. In this position he had firsthand knowledge of what the effects of catastrophic weather could be and how it might affect reunification. Late in the summer, a devastating typhoon rolled over the northern countryside, causing widespread flooding that destroyed hundreds of farms and homes and left thousands destitute. Crops suffered heavy damage. Inter-Korean relations warmed. Pyongyang accepted relief goods, food, clothing, and fuel from its neighbor. North Korea allowed home visits to performing artists and some family contacts. Nevertheless, the assassination attempt on President Chun the year before deterred any possibility of total reunification.

JUNE DEMOCRATIC STRUGGLE

The Burim case had nudged the young South Korean lawyer even deeper into the democratization movement. In 1985, Roh assumed the chairmanship of the Busan Citizens' Committee for Democracy. As chairman and director of the Busan headquarters of the People's Movement for a Democratic Constitution, he was forefront in the June democratization struggle. The protest remains an unsavory milestone in South Korean history, but ultimately it helped oust Chun's authoritarian regime and bring about constitutional revisions and democratic presidential elections.

Two years later, North Korea signed the Nuclear Non-Proliferation Treaty—its purpose to limit the spread of nuclear weapons. Nearly nineteen years before, the universal treaty had opened for signature. Currently there are 189 states that are part of the treaty. India and Pakistan have confirmed nuclear power, and Israel neither signed nor ratified the treaty. North Korea ratified the treaty, then violated it, and would later withdraw. The treaty was proposed by Ireland, and Finland was the first to sign. On May 11, 1995, by consensus, the parties to the treaty extended it indefinitely and without conditions.

Ratcheting up the news and thrusting Roh Moo Hyun into the political spotlight was an accident at Daewoo Shipping. A worker hit with fragments of exploding tear gas during a protest at the company's South Korean plant died. On behalf of the deceased man's family, Roh took the case. According to Roh, the government pressed false charges against him. Subsequently he was arrested and spent three weeks in jail for "aiding and abetting" striking workers, and his law license was suspended. Now the question was, would Roh's good intentions for a democratic government stop cold? Or could he recover and attain the success and power that he clearly craved?

Angry members from labor unions of numerous South Korean conglomerates protested for the right to elect their own leaders and to form outside the framework of the government

REUNIFICATION HAD NEVER LEFT THE MINDS OF SOUTH KOREANS.

or of the controlled Federation of Korean Trade Unions. Only one union per company was recognized by the government, and strikes were monitored by riot police. In September 1988, Daewoo employees organized to demonstrate their complaints.

One argument focused on Daewoo and its original owner. Twenty years before, Kim Woo Chung borrowed $18,000 from his family and friends to start a small trading company. For years, Kim was said to work fourteen hours a day, all year, building his company. Like Hyundai, Daewoo Shipping was an original *chaebol*, a powerful and independent family-owned conglomerate assisted by low-interest government funding. Chaebols played major roles in spearheading the South Korean economy. But large conglomerates also monopolized the sale of many products and were known for blatant nepotism. Chairmen of the boards shared top-level management with relatives rather than with those more qualified. Nepotism and excessive consumption by the wealthy offended many Koreans with a sense of Confucian austerity. Daewoo, one of the fastest growing conglomerates in South Korean history, was aided handsomely by the government in power.

DAMAGING INCIDENT

Reunification had never left the minds of South Koreans. Had it not been for the unexpected bombing of a Korean airliner, perhaps the doors of reunification, or even reconciliation between the North and South, may have opened. As it happened, any significant inroads between the two countries again deteriorated. Korean Air Flight 858 disappeared off Burma over the Indian Ocean in November 1987 with 115 passengers on board. South Korean officials claimed North Korean agents had planted a bomb that destroyed the aircraft, killing everyone on board.

ROH ELECTED TO THE NATIONAL ASSEMBLY

After Roh's unsuccessful involvement in Daewoo, his legal practice appeared shattered. A lifelong fighter for democracy and human rights, Roh did not give in to dictatorial or corrupt regimes. He entered and won the parliamentary election on the opposition Unification Democratic Party ticket and became a member of the thirteenth National Assembly. Members elected by popular vote held 276 seats and served four-year terms. Another 92 seats were appointed by political parties based on the respective share of the popular vote.

An ad hoc committee was appointed to investigate corruption charges of the Fifth Republic. Dozens of witnesses were called to testify against the Chun government. This was Roh's chance to move upward. During the hearings, he impressed the Korean public with his incisive lines and no-holds-barred interrogations of former officials. Televised accounts dazzled the public with revelations concerning suppression of the media, extortion of political funds from large corporations, and improprieties connected with the Ilhae Institute, a charitable foundation established by former President Chun and his family. Roh rapidly emerged as an influential figure in South Korean politics and gained a wide television audience of supporters.

A NEW PRESIDENT AND THE 1988 SUMMER OLYMPIC GAMES

In a New Year's interview, President-elect Roh Tae Woo outlined his political goals. Handpicked by his predecessor, he regretfully made remarks that echoed the authoritarian language of President Chun's 1987 New Year's speech. Roh Tae Woo called for "grand national harmony" to transcend political leadership and to see the country through, as well as "suprapartisan operation of national affairs, rooting out corruption, and if necessary, stern measures to bring leftist elements back into the fold." He promised to punish those guilty of past financial scandals,

After the multiparty democratic political system was instituted in South Korea, Roh Tae Woo *(above)* won the general election and stressed accountability in government. During his term, the 1988 Summer Olympics were held in Seoul, bringing international attention to South Korea and its investment potential.

to protect the press from harassment by law enforcement, to recognize intelligence agencies, to demilitarize politics, and to restore honor to victims of the Gwangju Massacre, according to the Web site country-studies.com.

Other leaders had their own agendas. In the general election on April 26, 1988, Kim Dae Jung's People's Party for Democracy (PPD) took the senior opposition position, which moved toward greater political independence. The chief justice of the Supreme Court resigned. Yi Il-kyu, also independent-minded, became chief justice, and thirteen new Supreme Court justices were appointed. The major shake-up had affected thirty-five senior district court and high court judges.

The administration had considered an ambitious policy called Nordpolitik based on the Federal Republic of Germany's Ostpolitik of the early 1970s Communist outreach. Seoul designed its own outreach version based on a self-reliant global posture, political democracy, more trade relations, and a demand for economic opportunities with China and the Soviet Union. Nordpolitik became the signature policy of President Roh Tae Woo and appeared responsible for the success of the 1988 Olympic Games.

SEOUL HOSTS 1988 OLYMPIC GAMES

"Peace, Harmony and Success" was the official slogan of the 1988 Summer Olympics, which became Seoul's impressive and worldwide diplomatic triumph. North and South Korea planned to cohost the games, but the Korean Air bombing had damaged the possibility. Nevertheless the Olympic Games went on to be a huge success. The international event helped South Korea establish diplomatic relations with 133 countries and establish 138 diplomatic missions, including consulate offices in Moscow. Seoul normalized relations with the People's Republic of China and the Soviet Union. Young athletes from North Korea, Cuba, and Ethiopia did not participate.

South Korea won 12 gold, 10 silver, and 11 bronze medals and ranked fourth overall. The Soviet Union took first place, East Germany second, and the United States third. The Olympic Committee allowed the host nation to add a sport. South Korea introduced tae kwon do, a stunning competition of kicking, sparring, and self-defense. (All Korean military units now are required to have a fourth dan black-belt degree in tae kwon do.)

The Seoul Olympics proved medals were not the only rewards garnered by the Soviets. When the Soviet team headed home, it brought back 36 South Korean televisions sets, 7 mini-buses, 4 large buses, 4 cars, and 1 copy machine—all gifts from Daewoo Shipping.

SOUTH KOREA AND THE UNITED NATIONS

Four decades before, the newly formed United Nations had sent troops to South Korea following a Communist assault that preempted the Korean War. In October of 1988, President Roh Tae Woo made his diplomatic debut as the first South Korean president to address the UN General Assembly (South Korea became a member in 1991).

President Roh Tae Woo called for a six-nation consultative conference to discuss a broad range of issues concerning peace, stability, progress, and prosperity in northeast Asia. He proposed replacing the existing 1953 armistice agreement with a peace treaty and pledged never to use force against North Korea. Pyongyang immediately shrugged off his proposal and flatly referred to Roh's motion as "old wine in a new bottle." The only statements acceptable to the North were the three basic principals for Korean reunification: reunification by peaceful means, reunification transcending ideological differences, and reunification without external interference. It was yet another stalemate.

5

Challenges
of the 1990s

FOR ROH MOO HYUN, THE 1990s WERE A TEST OF ENDURANCE AND FAITH.
The ambitious candidate, who compared himself to American
president Abraham Lincoln and his courageous struggle for
justice and democracy, faced his own Gettysburg. Like the sixteenth U.S. president, Roh refused to give up on his long-held
vision of democracy. For the South Korean people, it was a
decade of international diplomacy, survival, and government
corruption.

President Roh Tae Woo and the ruling DJP, in an effort to
overcome a weakened status in the National Assembly, managed to bring together both Kim Young-sam's RDP ruling
party and Kim Jong-pil's NDRP, according to Web site korea-
award.com. The three parties merged into the Democratic
Liberal Party to command a two-thirds majority in the leg-
islative body; it was a three-way political merger that rang of
stacking the deck.

In 1992, using his high-profile record in prodemocratic fronts, Roh Moo Hyun ran for the National Assembly representing his home base in the eastern district of Busan. With overwhelming hometown support, he won by a landslide. One year later, the young, liberal democrat lost his seat after quitting his party in protest of the three-party political merger. But it did not stop Roh from leading another political campaign to unite the opposition forces and to join Kim Dae Jung's run for president. Dedication to democratic values and dynamic speeches were not enough to block the solid three-way support of the newly merged parties. Roh Tae Woo's successor and collaborator, Kim Young-sam, won the election. Ironically, Kim was the first president in thirty years without a military background. During his term, South Korea established diplomatic relations with China, the nation's economy faltered, and uncertainty waged over the North's nuclear stand.

U.S. POSITION ON SOUTH AND NORTH KOREA

When U.S. secretary of defense Dick Cheney visited South Korea in February 1990, his intention was to mark a change in the status of the United States military presence. The United States would go from a leading position to a supporting role in South Korea's defense. Seoul was asked to increase its contribution to the enormous defense costs. In short, it was time for Seoul to stand on its own feet. The actions further appeared to avoid a potential American entanglement in the ongoing, complicated, and questionable South Korean politics.

In June, South Korea's Kim Young-sam and Soviet Union president Mikhail Gorbachev held their first summit in San Francisco. Some analysts asked, was this a way for the Soviets to use their growing economic power for political purposes and to distance themselves from Pyongyang? The answers appeared complex and unforthcoming. The two countires would meet again.

"YOU CAN ACHIEVE ANYTHING WHEN YOU KEEP ON TRYING WITH HOPE AND SELF-CONFIDENCE."

NUCLEAR ISSUE HAMPERS NEGOTIATIONS

Nine months later, the world was shaken when North Korea withdrew from the international Nuclear Non-Proliferation Treaty. Tensions and doubt ran at fever pitch. Yet three months later, North Korea suspended its withdrawal.

The next crisis arose in the summer of 1994, when North Korea's supreme leader, Kim Il Sung, died. "Our Dear Leader," as the North Koreans called him, was succeeded by his son, Kim Jong Il. The younger Kim had grown up in high luxury and was known to wear platform shoes and a bouffant hairdo to add to his small stature. How would his selfish lifestyle affect the impoverished North Korean people? Kim's personality was defined by CIA psychologist Jerrold Post in *Reader's Digest* of July 2007: Kim "can't really empathize with the pain and suffering of others—seemingly indifferent to three million deaths from starvation during a decade-long (and ongoing) famine, caused largely by his disastrous control of North Korea's economy."

ROH MOO HYUN VIEWS HIS LOSSES

After failing in a run for mayor of Busan in 1995, Roh was back in stride campaigning for a National Assembly seat in the Jongno district in Seoul, far north of his home base. No doubt he felt a deep sense of political defeat when he failed. However, Roh remained determined, his democratic vision unmarred. He noted, "As long as you have hope for the future and hope for anything for that matter, you can overcome any difficulty. Do not ever give up. You can achieve anything when you keep on trying with hope and self-confidence." And that is exactly what Roh did. He changed political course and joined the inner

South Koreans experienced a period of uncertainty when Kim Il Sung *(left)*, North Korea's leader, died suddenly in 1994. While the South Korean government did not always agree with Kim Il Sung, they knew what to expect from him. That was not the case with his son and successor, Kim Jong Il *(right)*, who was known for his love of luxury and excess.

circle of Kim Dae Jung's second campaign for president. Kim, too, failed.

In the uncertain hours of both Roh's and Kim's defeats, there must have been some consolation and satisfaction for their efforts in human rights and democracy. The conviction of two previous and notorious government officials finally had been accomplished. Former South Korean presidents Chun Doo Hwan and Roh Tae Woo were arrested on charges of corruption and financial influence, and they were imprisoned upon conviction in 1996. The Gwangju Massacre was recognized. May 18 was declared a National Day of Remembrance, and the May 18 Cemetery was sanctified. The government renounced the military definition of the uprising as a mob action and built the National Democracy Park, with an impressive memorial tower, exhibition rooms, and History Square. After Chun's release from prison, he tried to enter the park and was barred.

EMERGING POWER

In 1998, Roh's increased visibility and overwhelming efforts to overcome regionalism and warring political views provided him with an anchor position on radio news at Seoul Broadcasting Company. As a popular commentator, he was propelled to be elected to the fifteenth National Assembly in the Jongno district. Roh also served as arbitrator in a labor dispute at Hyundai Motors, South Korea's largest and the world's sixth largest auto maker.

Just weeks before the next presidential election, there was more adversity. Korea's economy collapsed as a result of the Asian financial crisis, and in the North, nature created its own disaster. Heavy rains and massive flooding caused power outages, food shortages, and major loss of lives. Thousands of North Koreans were left homeless and destitute. South Korea, the United States, and other nations came to the country's rescue, providing much-needed relief with food, clothing, and heavy fuel oil. Faced with huge and damaging losses, North Korea broke from its philosophy of self-reliance and accepted the aid. Still, over the next four years, between one million and three million North Koreans died of starvation.

KIM DAE JUNG ELECTED PRESIDENT OF SOUTH KOREA

Many thought Kim Dae Jung's political career was over when he lost in 1992 and took a hiatus to be a visiting scholar at Clare Hall, Cambridge University, in England. But when the Korean public revolted against the incumbent government of Kim Young-sam over the nation's financial losses and the collapse and scandal surrounding Hanbo Steel, it was time for him to return.

Roh Moo Hyun threw his support into Kim's fourth quest for president. In a razor-thin victory, Kim succeeded. Four days later, Chun Doo Hwan and Roh Tae Woo were released from prison and pardoned.

On February 25, 1998, Kim was inaugurated as the fifteenth president of the Republic of Korea, taking office with currency and stock values plummeting. Vigorously, he pushed for economic reforms, accepting a $57 billion bailout from the International Monetary Fund. Government subsidies to the elite conglomerates were dramatically cut or reduced. Kim announced the "Sunshine Policy" (similar to Nordpolitik) to improve relations with the North. At an unprecedented summit in Pyongyang on June 13, 2000, President Kim and North Korean leader Kim Jong Il agreed to work for reconciliation and eventual reunification of their two countries. On October 13, 2000, Kim Dae Jung was named the winner of the 2000 Nobel Peace Prize. Two years later, embarrassed by a naval clash with North Korea and by corruption probes targeting his family, Kim revamped his cabinet. He was credited by some with overseeing a recovery of the Asian financial crisis and with creating a fairer market for South Korea. In 2004, South

Korea became a member of the Organization for Economic Cooperation and Development and joined the "trillion dollar club" of world economics.

TALK OF PEACE

The United States, North Korea, South Korea, and China began four-way talks aimed at replacing the 1953 Armistice Agreement that ended the Korean War, with a permanent peace treaty. But the peace process was hindered by questions of who should sign the agreement and the presence of some 30,000 U.S. soldiers in South Korea. Without a solution to either problem, peace and reconciliation between the North and the South appeared doomed.

Then suddenly, North Korea unexpectedly fired a medium-range ballistic missile over Japan. Pyongyang arrogantly stated that they saw no reason why they should not test, develop, or deploy missiles as long as the United States technically had missiles in South Korea. Reluctantly, the United States responded that it would lift some economic sanctions against North Korea. One week later North Korea announced a halt in missile testing, according to the Center for Non-Proliferation Studies (CNS) in Monterey, California.

Roh had entered the race for the National Assembly from Seoul in 1998 and had won a two-year term. When the term ended, he returned to Busan and failed to win another National Assembly seat. Despite winning only two out of six elections, a grassroots groundswell kept him from quitting his failing political career. News of Roh's defeat prompted young supporters around the nation to form a fan club called Nosamo, which literally meant "people who love Roh Moo Hyun." With their digital campaign, Roh was appointed minister of Maritime Affairs and Fisheries from August to the following March. He also served as adviser and senior member of the Central Committee and appeared in a commercial for Daewoo Motors.

South Koreans became incensed and took to the streets after two U.S. soldiers were acquitted of charges stemming from an accident that resulted in the deaths of two Korean schoolgirls. Protestors burned flags *(above)* and waved banners demanding a decrease in U.S. interference in issues concerning the Korean peninsula.

PRESIDENT CLINTON DEMANDS NUCLEAR SHUTDOWN

When U.S. president Bill Clinton took office in 1993, he demanded North Korea shut down the Yongbyon nuclear reactor. According to Laura Bradford of *Time*, "The Pentagon drafted plans for strikes to take out North Korea's key nuclear-production sites. Pentagon officials say the plan has recently been reviewed and modified, but few believe any American President would ever authorize it."

Acute trans-Pacific negotiations and bargaining ensued until North Korea and the United States completed an "Agreed Framework" on October 21, 1994. North Korea agreed to freeze its nuclear program; to shut down the nuclear site, in exchange for assistance in building civilian nuclear reactors; to enact a step-by-step normalization of relations between the two nations; and to allow ad hoc inspections. North Korea would remain a party to the Nuclear Non-Proliferation Treaty.

U.S. secretary of state Madeleine Albright made the first official U.S. visit to North Korea in October of 2000. Presenting Kim Jong Il with a basketball signed by Michael Jordon, she was favored with two days of face-to-face discussions with the Korean ruler. Many South Koreans viewed her meeting as a prelude to ending 55 years of acrimony between North Korea and the United States. Afterward, perhaps as a sign of goodwill, 15 families were invited to visit relatives in the North and several major daily newspapers exchanged copies. There was talk of a cross-the-border rail line and a four-lane highway linking the two nations. But meetings between government ministers eroded. Unification ministry officials in Seoul said that the North's failed response could have been the result of Pyongyang's inability to deal with more than one thing at a time. "The North has proven in the past that it does not have the manpower necessary to promote exchanges with several partners at the same time," reported Jim Lea, Osan Bureau Chief.

In 2001, soon after Albright's visit, control of the U.S. Congress changed. The new Republican administration did not support the agreement. One side believed that the new North Korean leader agreed to a freeze primarily because of the U.S. agreement to phase out economic sanctions that had been in place since the Korean War. Others said that, because of congressional opposition, the United States failed to deliver on part of the agreement. Confidential minutes supporting the agreement have never been made public. The agreement largely broke down by 2003.

DESPITE DECADES OF IDEOLOGICAL ESTRANGEMENT, SOUTH KOREANS DID NOT WANT TO SEE ANY NUCLEAR ATTACK ON THEIR NORTHERN BROTHERS AND SISTERS.

GOING FROM BAD TO WORSE

When President George W. Bush assumed office in January 2001, he suspended diplomatic talks with North Korea and ordered a review of America's Korean policy. Six months later, Bush announced completion of the policy review, called "serious discussions and a broad agenda." North Korea refused to engage in talks with the United States and argued that the United States set unacceptable preconditions. At the end of the year, South Korea stated that the North possessed enough plutonium to construct one or two nuclear bombs, but it would take several years for the North to make the weapons. A year later, President Bush declared North Korea part of an "axis of evil" for developing weapons of mass destruction. Many South Koreans took the phrase to include all of Korea. Anti-American fervor rocked the country.

ROH MOO HYUN'S PRESIDENTIAL RUN

As Kim Dae Jung's term was running out, Roh stepped to bat. "During his run for presidency," CNN.com reported, "Roh campaigned on a pledge to heal labor conflicts and bridge the rivalry between his country's southeast and southwest, an ancient rift that sometimes seems only slightly less bitter than the enmity between South Korea and communist North Korea." But regional rancor had a sister. After Pyongyang acknowledged it was actively pursuing a nuclear-weapons program, Roh, the dark-horse candidate in a field of 11, also campaigned on a willingness to negotiate with the North.

Many South Koreans did not regard North Korea's nuclear-weapons program as a threat but as a deterrent against a U.S. attack on the North. Despite decades of ideological estrangement, South Koreans did not want to see any nuclear attack on their northern brothers and sisters. Such an attack would have had unspeakably adverse effects on the South, as well as a severe anti-U.S. backlash. The *Asian Times*, on February 2, 2007, recalled the tragedy of history: "The historical precedent of the United States dropping two atomic bombs on Japan had shown that another U.S. nuclear attack on another Asian adversary is not unthinkable—unless North Korea developed an effective nuclear deterrence." It was no wonder the peninsula trembled.

In September 2002, for the first time since the Korean War, North and South defense ministry officials engaged in official talks. According to Donald Macintyre in an article for *Time* magazine on December 2, 2002, presidential candidate Roh "says South Korea's security can be assured by continuing Kim's policies [the Sunshine Policy]. He wants to press Pyongyang to dismantle its atomic-weapons program without halting the flow of public and private money from Seoul, which amounts to about $250 million annually." Roh's opponent, Lee Hoi Chang, "prefers the stick to the carrot, and would halt assistance until the crisis is resolved. 'What has (Sunshine Policy) brought us?' he asks. 'It has brought us nuclear weapons.'" Macintyre continued, "At the moment, however, standing shoulder-to-shoulder with the U.S. is not where you want to be if you are running for office in South Korea. The country is currently embroiled in one of its periodic bouts of anti-American fervor, inflamed by the acquittal last month of two U.S. soldiers on trial for negligent homicide for running over two young Korean girls with an armored vehicle. U.S. officials have tried to ease tensions with numerous expressions of regret, including an apology by President Bush himself last Wednesday. But demonstrations show no signs of abating. On Nov. 26, at least 10 firebombs were thrown into a U.S. military compound in Seoul."

Macintyre went on to say, "The violence expresses a growing belief that the country no longer needs 37,000 U.S. troops stationed in South Korea. . . . Roh has taken just such a position in the past. But Lee, instead of scoring political points by emphasizing just how dangerous Kim Jong Il remains is forced to play the moderate. The cold warriors in his party can only hope that toning down the rhetoric will widen Lee's appeal and win him the election. Only then will they be able to test the theory that the North Korean question can be answered by a little less sunshine and a lot more stick."

NOSAMO YOUTH AID PRESIDENTIAL WIN

Roh Moo Hyun, the most progressive candidate to date, won the presidency on the Millennium Democratic Party (MDP) ticket by a clear majority. The December 12, 2002, South Korean presidential election marked an advancement in the country's ongoing process of democratization that began in the mid-1980s. Amid the changing political climate, Roh Moo Hyun's victory resulted from popular support encouraged by Nosamo—volunteers who organized themselves through the Internet and new technologies. Chang, Roh's opponent, had solid support from most of the conservative newspapers that dominated the nation. But Nosamo's digital savvy successfully attracted attention and turned public support to Roh Moo Hyun.

On polling day, Nosamo members, joined by other young campaigners, launched an extensive mobile-phone campaign encouraging friends to come out and cast votes. And out they came. Thousands of young people crowded into the polling booths. Afterward it was widely accepted that Roh's victory owed much to the use of the new media. Alternative information channels on the Web also proved to be an effective counter to mainstream journalism. Nosamo, inspired by courage and commitment for democracy and human rights, became the first political fan club to elect a president.

President Roh, according to Online NewsHour's profile of him, wrote that he wanted to be "'a leader who is always within reach of the people,' the type of president that went out without bodyguards to visit the markets and have a drink with the people."

6

The Sixteenth President of South Korea

WEEKS BEFORE PRESIDENT-ELECT ROH MOO HYUN TOOK OFFICE, ANTHONY Spaeth, in *Time*, reported, "He has chosen to make public appearances dressed in a *hanbok*, the traditional Korean baggy formal wear—a nationalistic gesture that seems weirdly mistimed. 'He wants to convince the U.S. that Korea is no longer a weak, postwar country that some people envision it to be,' says one of his advisers. 'The U.S. needs to meet him halfway.' . . . The Bush team is waiting for Roh to take the first step on that road. 'I don't think [the Bush Administration] is at all happy with the new regime,' says Selig Harrison, director of the National Security Project at Washington's Center for International Policy. 'They are very disturbed. But they don't want the South Korean–U.S. alliance unraveling, so the two sides are talking.' Talking is good—now the two sides have to start communicating."

73

Most analysts agreed that Roh's first challenge would be how to mend the country's relationship with the United States.

When Roh Moo Hyun became sixteenth president of South Korea, like the sixteenth president of the United States, Abraham Lincoln, he faced a country divided, a wavering economy, and sharp criticism from the media. In the past, South Korea had a record of civil disobedience, nepotism, corruption, anti-Americanism, and dictatorial regimes—hardly palatable issues for new leadership. Challenges confronted him: Korea's dynamic growth, the bilateral agreement with the United States that established the legal rights and responsibilities of U.S. troops in Korea, and the precarious nuclear situation. Most analysts agreed that Roh's first challenge would be how to mend the country's relationship with the United States.

Days prior to Roh's inauguration, Romesh Ratnesar wrote in *Time*, "The CIA isn't sure the North Koreans have the skill to make a nuclear device small enough to load onto its missiles. But, if they do, the danger is great. Pyongyang wields a huge stash of short- and medium-range missiles, including at least 100 Nodong missiles capable of striking Japan. . . . Pyongyang wants to become the first rogue state capable of striking the U.S. homeland with a missile. In 1998 the North Koreans test-fired a three-stage Taepo Dong-1 rocket that landed in the Pacific Ocean. The Pentagon believes that North Korea is developing an intercontinental ballistic missile . . . that could reach Alaska, Hawaii and possibly California. The North Koreans had pledged not to test-fire any long-range weapons until this year. If testing resumes, a U.S. military official says, Pyongyang may be able to target the continental U.S. with a nuclear warhead 'within several years.'"

For many South Koreans, Roh's success gave new hope for democratic values. "Equality and freedom will be much more respected in the practice of politics specifically, and in the daily life of Korean society," wrote Jaewoo Choo in the *Asia Times*, December 24, 2002.

Choo added, "What really appealed to those who have longed for change in Korea's political culture were Roh's vision and principles. Koreans were simply fed up with regionalism, cronyism and nepotism. They want a new Korea where common sense, democratic principles, and rule of law will prevail and perpetuate in both domestic and foreign life. Whether Roh is capable of fulfilling this desire remains to be seen."

Thus the poor country boy, born in a village of clay and thatched-roofed farmhouses, assumed the highest government seat of the Republic of Korea. According to Ray Suarez in Online Newshour, "In his inaugural speech, President Roh conceded that North Korea is a global threat, while sticking to his position that dialogue, not military action, is the safest way out." Roh said, "North Korea's nuclear development can never be condoned. Pyongyang must abandon nuclear development. If it renounces its nuclear development program, the international community will offer many things that it wants. It is up to Pyongyang whether it goes ahead and obtains nuclear weapons or gets guarantees for the security of its regime and international economic support."

The many dignitaries attending his inauguration included Japanese prime minister Junichiro Koizumi and U.S. secretary of state Colin Powell, who was touring East Asia. North Korea's Kim Jong Il had called for talks between South Korea and the United States. Powell responded that President Bush "believes strongly that multilateral talks are the appropriate way to begin to resolve this difficult issue. . . . It is not just a matter that concerns South Korea, North Korea and the United States. It is a matter that concerns Japan . . . the International Atomic Energy Agency . . . and the international community," according to Online NewsHour, reporting on Colin Powell's mission to Asia. Previously, China "had rebuffed Powell's proposal for

In the weeks leading up to his inauguration, President Roh Moo Hyun set out to forge relationships with the United States while persuading anti-American protestors to vacate the streets of Seoul. During his inaugural speech *(above)*, Roh promised to continue pacifist diplomacy with North Korea, despite reports of their nuclear testing mere hours before the ceremony.

a regional coalition to pressure North Korea to end its nuclear weapons program."

One almost could feel sympathetic for the new president's position, one that he had worked for years to attain. Yet President Lincoln had had severe critics and bold supporters too, and at that moment in history the Civil War was as towering as the current nuclear issue.

A NEW TAKEOFF TOWARD AN AGE OF PEACE AND PROSPERITY

President Roh was quick to lay out three major national policy goals. As stated by the president's Seoul office, he announced the "establishment of participatory democracy, balanced development of society, and the opening of a new era for a peaceful and prosperous Northeast Asia. The last issue," he said, "has served as the backbone of my government's foreign policy—an attempt to build a Northeast Asian community through a new regional order of cooperation and integration which transcends old antagonisms and conflicts among countries of this region." He stressed that the third policy "was vital for our survival and enhancing our prosperity."

Before the National Assembly, Roh stressed, "Pyongyang must abandon nuclear development," and he emphasized that confrontation was not the way to deal with the North. "Military tension in any form should not be heightened," he said.

Aside from the nuclear issue, peace and prosperity clung to South Korea's long and painful relationship with Japan. Concern about "the nuclear issue is the biggest stumbling block," Roh repeated, but he reiterated his hope that Japan would act decisively to resolve its wartime history "and appeal to its own conscience and rational wisdom." Roh was speaking of an ongoing series of actions in which Japan had justified its airbrushing of history textbooks regarding territorial sovereignty over Korea and its Dokdo Islets, the huge number of Korean women forced into sexual slavery during World War

II, and the controversial and reoccurring tribute by Japanese cabinet members at the Yasukuni Shrine.

The Yasukuni Shrine

The Yasukuni Shrine, a controversial monument in Tokyo, is dedicated to the spirits of soldiers and others who died fighting for the emperor of Japan, particularly to those killed in wartime. In October 2004, its Book of Souls listed the names of 2,466,532 men and women, including 27,863 Taiwanese and 21,181 Koreans, whose lives were dedicated to the service of imperial Japan. Included in the Book of Souls are 1,068 people convicted of war crimes by a post–World War II court, and a total of 12 convicted and 2 suspected Class A war criminals (for crimes against peace). The shrine's history museum contains an account of Japan's glorious actions in World War II. Despite protests, former prime minister Junichiro Koizumi made annual visits from 2001 to 2006 and bowed before the shrine. South Koreans had seethed at the very thought.

The Dokdo Islets

The Dokdo islets consist of several rocky peaks, 46 acres in all, that stick up in the middle of the Sea of Japan—or, as Korea calls it, the East Sea. The islands' main uses are fishing and bird watching. Speculation suggests there are natural gas reserves in water surrounding the islands. Both South Korea, which currently controls the islets, and Japan claim the Liancourt Rocks, a name that comes from the French whaling ship *Liancourt*, which charted the islets in 1849. North Korea refers to them as Tok Islet and supports control of the islands by "the Korean nation." South Korea claims the territory from records dated to the sixth century during the kingdom of Silla. The 1900 Korean Empire ordinance officially incorporated three islands into modern Ulleung County, North Gyeongsang. Japan's claims come from seventeenth-century records, as well as a *terra nullius* (no man's land) incorporation in 1905, as part of Okinoshima, in Oki District, Shimane Prefecture.

The rocks are composed mainly of two islets; 90 others are reefs and volcanic rocks. A Korean geologist reported that the eastern islet formed 4.5 million years ago. The island of Ulleungdo formed 2 million years later. The islets are 134 miles (217 km) from mainland Korea and 155 miles (250 km) from mainland Japan.

Over 900 Korean citizens list the islets as their residence, while over 2,000 Japanese do the same. However, only two people—a Korean couple—are actual permanent residents. Korean telecom service providers installed stations on the rocks to cover the islets in the South Korean wireless telephone network.

Approximately 37 South Korean policemen and policewomen guard the islets. There also is personnel from the Ministry of Maritime Affairs and Fisheries, a Korean couple whose occupation is fishing, and three lighthouse keepers who live in rotation. Before Roh Moo Hyun was president, he was minister of Maritime Affairs and Fisheries and showed unique knowledge and concern for the islets. From 1947 to 1952, the United States occupied the islets, using the area as a bombing range. As a result of military maneuvers, at least 30 Koreans were killed.

PRESIDENTS ROH AND BUSH CONVENE

Perhaps first and most important, President Roh visited the United States for a summit with President George W. Bush. May 2003 marked the fiftieth anniversary of the U.S.-ROK Mutual Defense Treaty, the dynamic alliance for continued peace and prosperity on the Korean Peninsula and in northeast Asia. Both world leaders discussed the importance of this agreement and pledged to work together to promote the values of democracy, human rights, and the market economy. They agreed to work out plans to consolidate key U.S. forces and to relocate the Yongbyon Garrison at an early date.

Roh Moo Hyun met with President George W. Bush *(right)* in 2003 to discuss U.S.–South Korean treaties and the handling of North Korea. Both leaders stressed the need for international involvement in helping defuse the nuclear crisis among the United States, South Korea, and North Korea and invited China and Russia to participate in negotiations.

The presidents noted the opportunity provided by Korea's growing national strength to continue the expansion of ROK armed forces in defending the peninsula and on international security challenges.

President Bush thanked President Roh for his country's military support in Iraq and the deployment of medical and construction units. Other efforts were to assist with post-conflict humanitarian assistance and reconstruction in Iraq.

North Korea's nuclear-weapons program was a major concern. Both leaders stressed that escalatory moves would only lead to the nation's greater isolation. Included in their talks was a strong commitment to work for complete, verifiable, and irreversible elimination of the North's nuclear program through peaceful means. Bush pointed out that China's recent role in the trilateral talks with South Korea and Japan was essential for a successful and comprehensive settlement. Russia and other nations also could play a constructive role in multilateral diplomacy.

As the United States and South Korea are leading donors of humanitarian food assistance to North Korea, both presidents agreed to lend assistance without linkage to political developments and stressed the need to ensure that assistance goes to those in need. Bush noted that North Korea's nuclear program stood in the way of humanitarian aid for its people. Roh agreed that his Peace and Prosperity Policy for a South–North reconciliation and future inter-Korean exchanges, or developments of the nuclear issue, would be conducted in trilateral consultations with Japan—essential terms Colin Powell previously had pointed out.

According to a White House press release, other topics included the International Thermonuclear Experimental Reactor (ITER) project, the Global Forum on Corruption, and efforts to improve the environment and to combat global crime and infectious diseases. The summit concluded with both presidents agreeing that their frequent telephone calls since Roh's election, as well as their substantial discussion in Washington, had enhanced mutual trust and respect.

President Roh and First Lady Kwon later met with leaders of the American Chamber of Commerce and the New

York Stock Exchange. They greeted members of the Korean Veterans' Association; toured the site of the World Trade Center, scene of the 9/11 terrorist attack; and met with leaders at the United Nations' headquarters. In Washington, D.C., they saluted fallen heroes in Arlington National Cemetery. At the Lincoln Memorial, Roh lauded Abraham Lincoln for promoting democracy and human rights. Lincoln had realized that reconciliation and the consolidation of American society were necessary at the time of the Civil War. This ideology coincided with Roh's election promises.

SHARP CRITICISM BACK HOME

Roh's meeting with President Bush was criticized by the South Korean people. The *Korea Herald* reported that Roh's statements during his U.S. visit took a dramatic turn from his past comments emphasizing an independent stance. Many Roh supporters expressed their anger with his pro-American remarks, denouncing them as a departure from his professed principles and as a threat to inter-Korean relations. Had Roh chosen a realistic solution to the North Korean issue to secure national interests, based on the acknowledgment of U.S. power? His young supporters condemned him for "kowtowing" to the U.S. president. Roh defended his turnaround toward the United States as "necessary to fit reality."

During the twenty-third anniversary of the prodemocracy civic uprising in Gwangju, 100 students at Chonnam National University shouted slogans denouncing Roh's pro-American statements. During his university lecture he replied, "You may have something to criticize about the United States but the reality required me to forge friendly ties between South Korea and the U.S. South Korea–U.S. relations should go on smoothly in the coming period." Roh added that he had been concerned that a rift between Seoul and Washington could heighten tension on the peninsula and complicate the relationship between him and the South Korean people. "It was the most urgent task to lay the groundwork for solving problems by settling concerns about the South Korea–U.S. alliance and economic uncertainties stemming from such concerns." Roh believed he had changed his thinking and concluded, "A president is required at every moment to make a choice," according to the Web site Kanaka in Korea: Hawaii and Korea Gateway.

7

Triumph Over Impeachment

THE WORLD SPOTLIGHT CAST GLOOMY SHADOWS ON THE SOUTH KOREAN presidency: scandal, corruption, a postage stamp controversy, and the National Assembly agreement to deploy 3,000 troops to the northern city of Kirkuk in Iraq.

"Our demands and those of the United States were in accord," said National Security adviser Ra Jong-yil, referring to the visit of a South Korean delegation to Washington to finalize troop deployment details. Seoul favored Kirkuk, Iraq's northern oil hub, for its good infrastructure and relative stability and safety from attacks. Reporters were told it would take about 16 weeks to assemble, train, and transport the troops, who would join the 675 medical and engineering personnel already there. The Korean contingent was expected to cost $200 million. This would make South Korea the third largest contributor to coalition forces after the United States and Great Britain.

According to a Web memo published by the Heritage Foundation, "This was an important political victory for President Roh Moo Hyun, whose leadership had been tested in recent months by waning public support and an antagonistic legislature." Although Roh's opposition party supported the deployment and decision to commit troops to Iraq, hundreds of protesters staged a riot.

THE DOKDO STAMP CONTROVERSY

The issue of a Dokdo postage stamp in Korea created a furor in Japan. Within three hours after the first issue, 1,874,000 stamps were sold out in Seoul. Across the country at post offices, people lined up to buy another 28,000 stamps. Japan countered that it would issue a Dokdo stamp of its own.

Both nations claimed possession of the Dokdo Islets in the Korean Straits, referred to as the Liancourt Rocks. In the 1954 Mutual Defense Pact with South Korea, the United States stated it would only go to Korea's aid in areas the United States recognized as lawfully Korean domain. The Dokdo Islets were not recognized by either Japan or Korea—it remains a disputed claim.

WHISPERING PRINCESS

If Roh thought being president would be smooth, Korean movies were a visual contradiction. As an example of explosive story content, consider a movie review written by James Brooke, of the New York Times News Service, of *Whispering Princess.* "The daughter of North Korea's leader, Kim Jong Il, is pouting in the suite of a luxury hotel in Seoul. She has just learned that Daddy has arranged a marriage for her in Pyongyang to a boring old nuclear scientist. Not for the Dear Leader's teenage princess! Donning a tight white blouse and a hot-red miniskirt, she eludes her amiable North Korean police chaperone and runs away to a disco, where she shouts in English, 'Let's party!' All goes swimmingly until the Americans, dressed in black, arrive

Roh, under pressure for involvement in illegal funds, was accused of receiving up to $6 billion during his presidential campaign.

at a rock concert. As the princess kisses a hunky Seoul rocker with a unification ballad reaching a crescendo, the Americans blow up the place with hand grenades and rocket launchers."

Korean filmmaker Peter Lee commented, "Actually, I like the U.S. I visit the U.S. two times a year."

IMPEACHMENT

Scandal and government corruption are not new to Korea. History relates deeply embedded incidents where leaders participated in huge pay-to-play games. But impeachment was a first. While its reasons now appear petty, on March 14, 2004, the impeachment of President Roh was anything but trivial.

The previous December, President Roh threatened to resign from office and quit politics if his presidential campaign fund surpassed a tenth of what the opposition GNP took in during the last presidential campaign. Roh, under pressure for involvement in illegal funds, was accused of receiving up to $6 billion during his presidential campaign. No doubt by threatening to resign, Roh hoped to turn the glare on his opposition. It was suggested the Grand National Party received illegal donations from the big chaebols in staggering amounts, such as $10 billion from Hyundai Motor Co., $15 billion from LG Group, and $14 billion from Samsung Group, among other conglomerates. South Korea's constitution exempts an incumbent president from being charged with criminal offenses, except those that affect national security. Roh agreed to cooperate with the investigation but not to volunteer information.

According to a *Korea Herald* editorial in March 2003, "When President Roh made up his cabinet, the first criterion

As opponents of Roh Moo Hyun pushed forth impeachment proceedings, the members of parliament who were loyal to the president struggled to physically prevent the vote from being called. While security guards protected the Speaker as he announced the results of the impeachment proceedings, various members hurled shoes and books at him *(above)*.

was a reformist vision. . . . Certainly, the president initially identified amateurism with reform mindedness and believed that he could lead an administration of people armed with nothing but youthful passion. But, unfortunately, some of his appointees, like Cheong Wa Dae, had to leave over corruption charges. . . ." The editorial further stated, "Roh instructed that leftover campaign funds for local elections in Busan, his hometown, be paid to Choi Do-sul. If the president did what he is accused of, it definitely constituted a criminal act. While it clearly implicated the president in these money deals, the prosecution said it decided not to investigate him because of the constitutional immunity clause and so as not to disturb the performance of his official duties."

Prosecutors claimed Roh's side took in about $11.2 woo billion (U.S. $9.4 million) from South Korean businesses. Roh disputed the claim. The GNP supposedly took in $84 woo billion (U.S. $72 million). With huge amounts of suspicious money on both sides, it was not campaign funds that caused Roh's impeachment but his vocal support for the URI Party (Our Open Party). South Korean law states that government officials in office must remain neutral. Roh had said leftover campaign funds should go to Choi Do-sul. A political battle ensued.

"As shocking as the impeachment was," commented Peter M. Beck of the *Jeju Times*, "almost equally distressing was the manner in which the impeachment vote took place. The America media was full of images of brawling politicians and flying shoes. The images reinforced the stereotype that Koreans are a hot-headed people. In order for Korea to join the ranks of advanced democracies, it is essential for Korea's political leaders to be able to settle their differences peacefully through the existing laws and institutions.

"Equally important," added Beck, "the Korean public faces the challenge of not letting the political strife lead to social strife. Koreans must show the maturity that was on display during the 2002 World Cup and the candlelight vigils for the two school girls killed during a U.S. military training exercise."

The impeachment proceedings started on March 9, 2003. Outside, Baek Eun-jeong, a 51-year-old member of Nosamo, set himself on fire, suffering burns over 40 percent of his

The charges brought forth during President Roh Moo Hyun's impeachment proceedings would be classified by most countries as trivial. With the opposition accusing Roh of misappropriating election funds, they were also pushing for his dismissal due to Roh's illegal endorsement of the URI party.

body; he was rushed to a hospital unconscious. A suicide note read, "No politician can have the right to reprimand President Roh." The next day Roh apologized for the public turmoil but did not apologize for the controversies over the slush funds or the intimated corporate scandals. Protesters in the streets of Seoul got out of hand and tragedy emerged. When President Roh went on national television and accused Nam

Sang-guk, the former president of Daewoo Engineering and Construction Company, of bribery, Nam committed suicide by jumping off a bridge into the Han River.

Chaos reigned inside the National Assembly building as political opponents geared up to vote on Roh's impeachment. Outside, several thousand Roh supporters demanded the motion be withdrawn. Not until the morning of March 12, when opposition lawmakers and security guards forcibly removed pro-Roh officials from the floor of the assembly, did members vote. The motion, violation of election law, passed 193–2 to impeach. Supporters from Nosamo demanded the motion be withdrawn and chanted, "No impeachment and no more political chaos."

The Roh team later claimed they were deprived of the right to vote. All members of the URI Party resigned from the National Assembly but rescinded their resignations 10 days later. Roh's powers were officially suspended at 5:15 P.M., March 12. Prime Minister Goh Kun assumed the reins of power. Damage to the country's reputation and national security seemed imminent.

"The most representative of President Roh's first two years in office was his triumph over impeachment and the enforced rearrangement of the capital relocation plan," wrote Chen Weimin in *Two Years of Roh Moo Hyun's Administration.* The general public had backed Roh as a "president of reform." In domestic politics he stood on the slogan of "breaking old-style politics" and pushed for economic reforms, benefits for the middle class, and fairer distribution of wealth. He reiterated his vow to maintain peace on the Korean Peninsula through reconciliation with the North. The political elite were angered and the opposition retaliated with numerous obstacles.

Roh was impeached on charges of violating election laws. Fallout ignited on all sides. The unpopular impeachment apparently had backfired. The following April, his party won a majority. They "urged the masses to riot" with biased

THE LONG-TERM IMPLICATIONS OF THE IMPEACHMENT REMAINED UNCLEAR, BUT FAR-REACHING NONETHELESS.

coverage of the impeachment, reported the *Seoul Times* on March 13, 2004. The Grand National Party argued that "One-sided reports by TV broadcasters were a serious problem and distorted democracy." Of South Korea's three major television networks, only the Seoul Broadcasting System was not state-owned.

On May 14, 163 days later, the Constitution Court overruled the presidential impeachment. This degree constituted a declaration that Roh's reform plans would be fully implemented. And so President Roh was victoriously reinstated with major domestic changes. This prompted international diplomatic trips to meet and be photographed with the world's powerful elites. The long-term implications of the impeachment remained unclear but far-reaching nonetheless.

STATE-CONTROLLED NEWSPAPERS

Major South Korean newspapers next attacked Roh over his decision to move the administrative capital from Seoul to the rural Yeongi-Kongju area, roughly 100 miles (160 km) to the south. Election-law scandals, high unemployment, and relations with North Korea made headlines.

Roh's response to relocating the capital was, "There is a huge development gap between Seoul and the provinces, hindering a balanced national development. Seoul's 12 million people are one-quarter of the country's total. Overpopulation contributes to serious economic and social problems," according to Roh's office.

Angered by continued media accusations, Roh sued the country's top four newspapers for civil defamation and disputed reports that accused him of making questionable real-estate investments. In June 2004, he dropped the charges. According to the *Seoul Times*, administration officials stated, "The president concluded that it is undesirable to go on with the suits while he is in office."

Growth of the Korean Internet served to aid Roh's dismantlement of the press-club system at the presidential offices. "The old system allowed a closed circle of reporters from major news outlets to set news coverage," he claimed, "sometimes in conjunction with government officials," the *Seoul Times* reported.

"According to a *Fortune* magazine survey, South Korea, with an estimated broadband penetration of 75 percent of the population, may be the world's most wired nation. . . . Many of the country's younger citizens, who constituted a formidable presence at the polls, received news exclusively from the Internet. While they grappled with issues of responsibility and ethics, they recruited 'citizen reporters' to cover the news and offered a rich diversity of perspectives that contrasted with the ideologically entrenched media establishment," according to the *Seoul Times*.

CHAPTER

8

"The Foolish Old Man"

ONCE A SHY YOUNG MAN FROM MEAGER BEGINNINGS, ROH NOW FACED A momentous challenge. Those years of defeat, struggle, and rebound had honed his dedication to human rights and democracy. As the sixteenth president of the Republic of Korea, he knew the next years would be his biggest test.

Chen Weimin wrote, "South Korea's existing political setup completely changed with new and democratic leadership. Not only was transformation from the old to the new realized, the Korean people longed for changes. They wanted to see an end to the malpractices of the old system, such as money, politics, embezzlement and corruption." President Roh was determined to declare war on the old system, with political battle cries of "participatory government, realizing transition from the old to the new, and breaking old-style politics and privileged politics which won over the people."

But Weimin added that in a period of transition from a "money democracy" to an "incorruptible/clean democracy" there were limitations. "The old forces, which are still strong and influential in Korea, will inevitably impede him in a variety of ways. The reforms Roh is pursuing are by no means easy ones."

In an interview with Chinese journalists, Roh described his system of government "in the spirit of The Foolish Old Man who moved mountains." His philosophical paraphrasing referred to an ancient Chinese fable popularized by Mao Tse-tung, former chairman of the Chinese Communist Party. On June 11, 1945, Mao compared the endurance and struggle of the Chinese Communists to that of the "foolish old man who moved mountains" and who built the People's Republic of China. A brief look at President Roh's speech shows that the fable invokes a similar likeness to Roh's goals. A portion of Mao's speech follows:

"Our aim in propagating the line of the congress is to build up the confidence of the whole Party and the entire people in the certain triumph of the revolution. . . . We must also arouse the political consciousness of the entire people so that they may willingly and gladly fight together with us for victory. We should fire the whole people with the conviction that China belongs not to the reactionaries but to the Chinese people. There is an ancient Chinese fable called 'The Foolish Old Man Who Removed the Mountains.' It tells of an old man who lived in northern China long, long ago and was known as the Foolish Old Man of North Mountain. His house faced south and beyond his doorway stood two great peaks, Taihang and Wangwu, that obstructed the way. He called his sons, and with hoe in hand they began to dig up these mountains with great determination. Another graybeard, known as the Wise Old Man, saw them and said derisively, 'How silly of you to do this! It is quite impossible for you few to dig up those two huge mountains.' The Foolish Old Man replied, 'When I die, my sons will carry on; when they die, there will be my grandsons, and then their sons and grandsons, and so on to infinity. High as they are, the mountains cannot grow any higher and with every bit we dig, they will be that much lower. Why can't we clear them away?' Having refuted the Wise Old Man's wrong view, he went on digging every day, unshaken in his conviction. God was moved by this, and he sent down two angels, who carried the mountains away on their backs. Today, two big mountains lie like a dead weight on the Chinese people. One is imperialism, the other is feudalism. The Chinese Communist Party has long made up its mind to dig them up. We must persevere and work unceasingly, and we, too, will touch God's heart. Our God is none other than the masses of the Chinese people. If they stand up and dig together with us, why can't these two mountains be cleared away?"

Indeed, the fable can mirror Korea's wretched past and the gigantic democratic goals President Roh sought.

TRAVELS ABROAD

Roh's democratic aims included improving foreign relations and strengthening friendly exchanges outside northeast Asia. Thus President Roh embarked on a world diplomatic tour. Accompanied by First Lady Kwon Yang-suk, Roh was generously feted by international heads of state.

In England, after attending the official welcoming ceremony at the Horse Guards, President Roh and First Lady Kwon rode in Queen Elizabeth's royal and gilded carriage to Buckingham Palace. At a state dinner, they appeared with the queen and Prince Philip. Queen Elizabeth and President Roh wore the royal red sashes that befit heads of state. In Warsaw, Poland, the president and first lady visited the Daewoo electronics factory, and in New Delhi, India, they scattered flower petals on Mohandas Gandhi's tomb at Gandhi Memorial Park. Roh shook hands with Indian prime minister Manmohan Singh. He held a summit with Russian president Vladimir

After his impeachment, Roh flew around the world and met with foreign dignitaries and politicians to bolster international relationships with South Korea. Along with his wife, First Lady Kwon Yang-suk, Roh toured Korean factories in Europe and even dined with the British royal family *(above)*.

Putin in the Kremlin. Greetings from the Republic of Korea were extended to Argentine president Nestor Kirchner. There were more summits with President Jacques Chirac of France and Japanese prime minister Junichiro Koizumi. After visiting Arlington National Cemetery in Washington, D.C., and after placing a wreath at the Korean War Memorial, there were several meetings with President George W. Bush.

A GREATER CHALLENGE

Two years into Roh's presidency, Professor Mark Peterson of Brigham Young University said, in *Two Years of Roh Moo Hyun's Administration,* "Mr. Roh's greatest challenge has been dealing with the American president over the U.S.-ROK alliance. Mr. Bush's unilateral moves in Korea have been a surprise to those who have watched the alliance since the Korean War. Secretary of Defense Donald Rumsfeld announced the unilateral withdrawal of American forces from forward positions (DMZ). In doing so, he nodded to the anti-American sentiment in the country, a remarkable retreat for such a seemingly strong secretary of defense."

Balbina Youngkyung Hwang, policy analyst for northeast Asia for the Asian Studies Center of the Heritage Foundation, U.S.A., said, "Increasingly, more and more dissatisfaction about the United States is being expressed in South Korea. Much of it unfortunately is cast as 'anti-American' sentiment. These views include calls to end the 'unfair' U.S.-ROK alliance, which is regarded by some as an impediment to the Korean people's desire and will to move towards independence and reunification.

"Second, and most severe, Mr. Bush has broken with South Korea in that he has begun to deal with North Korea independently. No longer do South Korea and the United States provide a united front to North Korea. This has been a huge political victory for North Korea.

"It is remarkable that under President Roh there is progress toward peace and reconciliation . . . in spite of the growing tension between North Korea and the United States. President Roh's greatest accomplishments thus far were his continued pursuit of peace with North Korea."

Li Xiangyang, deputy director of the Institute of World Economics and Politics Chinese Academy of the Social Sciences, gave President Roh high marks for his first two years of economic reform and corporate restructure.

His numerous meetings with world leaders, industrial giants, and members of the American Chamber of Commerce have contributed to his country's phenomenal growth.

Despite grueling, endless summits and local politics, there were lighter moments. President Roh and the first lady enjoyed meeting hundreds of overseas Korean children and their families during their round-the-world jaunts. Back home at the Children's Village in Seoul, the president was photographed chatting with smiling children and encouraging them to have hopes and ambitions. He told them a story of his impoverished life and difficult schooling when he was young. During one such visit, a photo taken appeared on a postage stamp commemorating Roh's inauguration.

Currently, the president's son, Roh Geon-ho, is an MBA student at Stanford University in California. Daughter Roh Jeong-yeon is employed by the embassy.

SOUTH KOREA'S FANTASTIC GROWTH

President's Roh's long-held vision of human rights and a democratic nation cannot be underscored by South Korea's global economics. His numerous meetings with world leaders, industrial giants, and members of the American Chamber of Commerce have contributed to his country's phenomenal growth. South Korea signed the first free-trade agreement with Chile in early 2005. This was expected to advance Korea's economic system, to enhance service sector competitiveness, and to attract more investment. Bilateral trade increased significantly with the administration reporting a 114.3 percent surge in its exports to Chile and a rise in its imports. Singapore and EFTA (European Free Trade Association) expanded more world logistics.

As a global hub for a number of multinational corporations, Singapore agreed to provide preferential tariff treatment to goods produced in South Korea's burgeoning Gaeseong Industrial Complex. These agreements benefited both countries' economies, reported South Korean government officials.

Negotiations continued with the United States for the establishment of an Asia-Pacific FTA (Free Trade Agreement). This alliance included commodities, agricultural products, financial services, telecommunication, investments, government procurements, and smoother access to each other's markets. This agreement is expected to reduce security risks and to increase Korea's international credibility and foreign investments.

President Roh was elected by an energetic and sophisticated digital campaign. South Korea ranked number one in the Digital Opportunity Index International Telecommunication Union (ITU), a leading international telecommunication organization. This ranking advanced South Korea's image with infrastructure products and mobile cellular subscribers, grew its mobile Internet subscribers, offered Internet access at home, and boosted the brand value of its companies.

The world's first digital multimedia broadcasting (DMB), which allows users to watch television through mobile devices, was launched during the 2005 Asian-Pacific Economic Cooperation (APEC) summit in Busan. Major leaders from 21 member countries attended the huge international event. President George W. Bush represented the United States. Meetings strengthened cooperation for the creation of an Asia-Pacific community. Members agreed to cooperate more closely in advancing free trade and in ensuring a safe Asia-Pacific region.

In 2005, inter-Korean trade reached a record U.S. $1 billion for the first time since bilateral trade began in 1989. Commerce with the North increased with exchanges in trade shows and products. Even without counting tourists to the North's Mt. Geumgang resort, nearly 90,000 North and South Koreans

Successful talks with North Korean officials are viewed as positive steps toward the reunification of the two Korean countries. Increased interaction between North and South Koreans also included reunions of separated families *(above)* who had not seen each other since before the Korean War.

visited each other. This was more than the total number of personal exchanges between the South and North during the previous six decades.

Roh, always passionate about helping socially vulnerable citizens, supported efforts to expand the social welfare budget, which

"ONLY WHEN INTEGRATION IS ACHIEVED, WILL THE REFORM OF THE NATION AND PROGRESS BE POSSIBLE."

resulted in raising the minimum cost of living by 8.9 percent. The increase provided the basis for determining who received social welfare benefits for living and medical expenses.

Roh endorsed the Ministry of Labor's plans to establish additional job centers for women and to increase the number of career development centers for female university students by 2010.

Finally, President Roh's constant effort to move the capital and widen the gap between Seoul's metropolitan area and its provincial areas was approved by the Constitutional Court. To have created a multifunctional administrative city and to have relocated public organizations to regional cities were immense accomplishments.

Mindful of President Abraham Lincoln's paraphrase of the biblical verse Matthew 12:25, "Every kingdom divided against itself is brought to desolation, and every city or house divided against itself shall not stand," Roh never lost sight of reunification. "Without first mending the rift between the eastern and western regions of Korea," he said, "it is impossible for the country to push ahead with reform and national reunification. Only when integration is achieved, will the reform of the nation and progress be possible."

North Korea's stubborn nuclear stance played a key role in the adoption of the September 19 Joint Statement, concluded during the fourth round of the Six-Party Talks. Accordingly, the foundation for a peaceful resolution and the establishment of a peaceful regime for the entire peninsula was spelled out.

The ancient tale of "The Foolish Old Man" and the profound thoughts of Abraham Lincoln appeared to come together.

9

Korea's Cultural Advances

OVER THE LAST 60 YEARS, THE NATIONAL MUSEUM OF KOREA HAS MOVED 7 times. Perhaps now it will never move again. In the last month of 2005, the world's sixth-largest museum opened in Seoul. Forty-five days later, one million visitors were reported to have viewed its ambitious grandeur. "The Asian Arts Gallery was created in order to offer an opportunity to experience the cultural diversity of Asia by exhibiting items from China, Japan, South East Asia, and Central Asia," said museum director Hongnam Kim. "Our goal is to create a world-class museum in Asia through active international cultural exchanges. The museum offers a variety of educational programs and recently opened a Children's Museum. The Young Theatre Hall provides gallery and theatrical experiences with musical performances, plays, and films."

ONE DAY IT COULD BE USED TO REUNITE FAMILIES SEPARATED AFTER THE 1952 TRUCE.

ALL ABOARD KTX

Keeping up with demands of international travelers, business-people, and residents, in 2004 South Korea launched the world's fifth high-speed railway; this one linked Seoul and Busan. The KTX express train reduced travel from more than four hours to two hours and forty minutes.

Streamlined like the shape of a shark's head, with bold, curved lines, the rail cars embody a unique Korean style. The sleek textured outer surface was processed to minimize air resistance. The train's huge source of power corresponds to approximately 18,200 horsepower. A high-speed railway linking Osong and Mokpo will be completed in 2017. The KTX is a remarkable accomplishment for South Koreans held under authoritarian regimes for so many years.

NORTH KOREA AND SOUTH KOREA RAILWAY LAUNCHED

When the Korean Peninsula was divided in 1945, the North/South Korean railway cut the peninsula in half. After the Korean War, all traces of the railroad were removed. In 2000, a plan to reconnect the two nations by rail was agreed upon. On September 13, 2003, the Trans-Korean railway was completed, linking North and South Korea. Its intended prime use is to carry freight, and it is envisaged that one day it could be used to reunite families separated after the 1952 truce.

The railway reduced transport costs by about a third and cut transit times in half. Both sides participated in the hazardous work. The North pledged to reconnect a 9.2 mile (14.8 km) section from Kaesong station to the DMZ in the north. The South restored a 1.1 mile (1.7 km) section in the DMZ. A two-lane road was constructed next to the single-track Kyungeui

The South Korean train KTX has become a symbol of the country's continuing modernization. Designed in the model of a shark's head, the speedy train has minimized travel time between cities, creating a more connected and unified South Korea.

railway, its main purpose being to allow for the clearing of hundreds of live land mines left after the Korean War, to make way for a safe corridor of railway and road traffic.

ROK-U.S. ALLIANCE BEGETS PRIORITY

In November 2005, President Roh and President George W. Bush met in Gyeongju to discuss the Joint Declaration of the ROK-U.S. Alliance and Peace on the Peninsula.

According to the White House's Office of the Press Secretary, "the alliance not only stands against foreign threats but also for the promotion of the common values of democracy, market economy, freedom, and human rights in Asia and around the world." Both presidents acknowledged the relocation of United States forces on Korean bases, including Yongbyon Garrison, and the partial reduction of U.S. forces in Korea.

Purposes of the alliance expressed by both parties were APEC's bilateral cooperation in the United Nations' fight in the global war on terror, and efforts to prevent proliferation of weapons of mass destruction and their means of global delivery. APEC also provides common ground for leaders to meet regularly to discuss current issues and resolve disputes.

According to the U.S. Department of State's International Information Programs Web site, "Roh and Bush also agreed to launch a strategic dialogue called Strategic Consultation for Allied Partnership (SCAP) at the ministerial level for consultations on bilateral, regional, and global issues of mutual interest. The two leaders agreed to hold the first strategic dialogue at the beginning of 2006."

While expressing confidence that a peaceful solution could be achieved, the presidents reiterated that a nuclear-armed North Korea will not be tolerated and reaffirmed that the nuclear issue should be resolved through peaceful and diplomatic means. North Korea must eliminate its nuclear weapons programs promptly and verifiably. Both agreed the September 19 Joint Statement was an important step toward a denuclearized North Korea and its commitment to abandon all nuclear weapons and existing nuclear programs.

According to White House press secretary Tony Snow, the most significant achievement was the fact that the two presidents had frank conversations and were able to develop mutual trust and respect on personal levels.

BUSAN HOSTS AN APEC MEETING

"I should note that Busan is my hometown. It is where I was schooled and brought into the world of politics. This is why I am awash with an excitement such as would animate a host inviting guests into his own doors," President Roh Moo Hyun proudly said at a gala dinner for APEC's economic leaders in 2005.

"Busan is Asia's gateway to the Pacific. Its ports are an unfailing beacon reaching out to an unending array of international events including Asia's largest film festival. Its friendly embrace will touch the hearts of all in our global village. No other venue is better suited for discussing the promising future of APEC." Seated at the head table next to the president were President Vladimir Putin of Russia and U.S. president George W. Bush and his wife, Laura.

"For talking face to face," concluded Roh, "leads to deepening understanding and greater bonds of trust. It paves the ways where none were to be seen, and inspires hope when hope seemed distant. This alone should suffice to speak for APEC's success. The Republic of Korea was able to achieve rapid growth and advance its democracy with nourishment from the global community. We will be equally unstinting in our commitment to developing APEC."

The original APEC forum was held at Blake Island, Washington, in 1989. The Republic of Korea was a founding member. Currently there are 21 members. By the end of the century, Seoul had ranked as the world's tenth-largest trading nation in the world.

AN UNFAIR ALLIANCE?

"Many begin to wonder if the marriage is over," wrote Balbina Youngkyung Hwang in *Transforming the U.S.–ROK Alliance into a 21st Century Relationship.* "Increasingly more and more dissatisfaction with the United States is being expressed in South Korea, much of it unfortunately cast as 'anti American' sentiment. These views include calls to end the 'unfair' U.S.-ROK Alliance, regarded by some as an impediment to the Korean people's desire, and a will to move towards independence and reunification.

"It is in America's interest," Hwang said in reference to the Busan summit, "to maintain the balance of power in Asia." But, she added, "It requires both Washington and Seoul to take a hard look at what their future strategy and vision for the region is. Alliances may be borne from the sharing of common interests, but bilateral relationships prosper on more: the sharing of common values."

The ROK-U.S. Alliance celebrated its fiftieth anniversary in 2003 and was the result of the Korean War and the division of the Korean Peninsula. Nearly 1.8 million Americans went to Korea, and 37,000 were killed. Fifty thousand South Korean troops served in Vietnam, and more than 4,400 lost their lives "to pay back the debt they owed to America," wrote Hwang. More recently, 5,000 South Koreans have served in Afghanistan and Iraq.

Payback and bilateral negotiations are complex and far-reaching. Consider the dollars spent between the two countries: trade between the two nations reached U.S. $69 billion in 2000. Since 1962, the United States has invested nearly U.S. $27 billion in assets in South Korea, with nearly U.S. $4.5 billion invested in 2002 alone. South Korean investments in the United States since 1968 have reached over U.S. $14 billion with over U.S. $1.3 billion invested in 2002. American firms exported U.S. $22.6 billion in 2002 to South Korea.

SIX-PARTY TALKS

South Korea played an active role in the adoption of the September 19 Joint Statement that led to the foundation for the peaceful resolution of the North Korean nuclear issue. The fifth round of talks concerned the stable management of the nuclear issue.

During the 2007 six-party talks concerning the North Korean nuclear program, delegates from the United States and Japan agreed to take steps toward normalizing relations with North Korea. The meeting's South Korean participants reconfirmed their commitment to providing electric power to the Communist country.

Members of the Six-Party Talks were North Korea, South Korea, the United States, Japan, Russia, and China. Their mission: to promote economic cooperation in the fields of energy, trade, and investment in the region. During the fifth meeting, they issued a joint statement: The DPRK is committed to abandoning all nuclear weapons and existing nuclear programs and returning, at an early date, to the Treaty of the Non-Proliferation of Nuclear Weapons and IAEA safeguards. North Korea responded that it had the right to peaceful uses of nuclear energy. The United States and North Korea agreed to respect each other's sovereignty, to exist peacefully together, and to take steps to normalize their relations. Japan and North Korea took steps to normalize their relations to settle the unfortunate past and other issues of concern. South Korea confirmed its proposal of July 12 concerning the provision of 2 million kilowatts of electric power for the North.

For 19 years, the government sought to resolve the issue of South Korea's nuclear waste. In November 2005, the Roh administration reported that, after nearly two decades of discussions, a disposal site was successfully selected through residents' votes in Gyeongju. The government agreed to install safety measures to separate low- and intermediate-level wastes from spent nuclear fuel and to provide special grants for the host city. Korea Hydro & Nuclear Power Company's head office moved to the host region.

THE KOREAN ENTERTAINMENT INDUSTRY

While President Roh and his administration were knee-deep in decisive world affairs and complex issues of running a democratic regime, the South Korean entertainment industry challenged world media acclaim with record ticket sales.

A satirical monster movie called *The Host* attracted more than 13 million viewers, setting a box-office record. An estimated 3 million rated DVDs of the movie were sold in China. Another 280 Chinese screens ran *The Host* and within one week grossed $670,000 woo in ticket sales.

Directed by Bong Jun-ho, the movie tells the story of a family's struggle to rescue a terrified daughter taken by a mutant monster that lurks in Seoul's Han River. Superb computer graphics enhanced its storyline.

Kim Duk-soo, a master of traditional Korean music, celebrated fifty years in entertainment with special performances at Seoul's Sejong Center for the Performing Arts. In 1959, as a member of the traveling musical troupe known as Namsadang,

Kim won the President's Award at the National Fold Music Concert. In 1978, he formed the Kim Duk-soo Samulnori Troupe with a new twist—traditional music played with four traditional percussion instruments called *samulnori.*

To commemorate his long and successful career, the Korean Ministry of Culture and Tourism presented Kim with an award in recognition of his work to promote traditional Korean arts.

The Last Empress, a story of Queen Min, the last queen of Korea's Joseon dynasty, topped one million viewers—the first time a Korean-created musical attracted theatergoers in such large numbers. Legend recalled that Queen Min struggled against her political enemies and Japan's imperial ambitions. In 1895, she was hacked to death by Japanese assassins and burned on the grounds of Seoul's main palace.

The musical was first performed in 1995, the one hundredth anniversary of Queen Min's murder. Since then it has been staged nearly 800 times. *The Last Empress* was the first musical from East Asia to be presented in London's West End and on New York's Broadway. The *New York Times* and the *Daily Telegraph* gave high praise to the musical production.

Sports are greatly loved in Korea. Lee Kang-seok and Nam Hyun-hee set all-time athletic records in two very different sports. Lee Kang-seok became the world's fastest man on ice, setting a world record for the 500 meters at the 2007 World Single Distances Speed Skating Championships in Salt Lake City, Utah.

In March 2004, 25-year-old Nam Hyun-hee became the first Korean fencer to be ranked number one in the world, according to the Federation Internationale d'Escrime, the international governing body of fencing.

Park Tae-hwan celebrated his victory in the men's 400m freestyle final at the World Swimming Championship in Melbourne, Australia, on March 25, 2006, and he became the first Korean to win a world title in swimming.

10

Legacy of Roh Moo Hyun

IN 2007, A VOLLEY OF INTERNAL AND WORLD CHALLENGES DOMINATED Roh's final months in office. In March, he supported the "Participatory Government's" identification of 10 promising industries: digital TV/broadcasting, intelligent robots, hybrid autos, intelligent model-home networking, digital content/SW solutions, display devices, biomedicine, next generation batteries, semiconductors, and mobile communications. Sound futuristic and insurmountable? Remember that it was Nosamo's digital campaign that helped Roh get elected.

At the forty-second commencement ceremony of the Korean Third Military Academy, Roh was upbeat. "Around the time I took office, the country was faced with difficult choices to make on major issues—the North Korean nuclear problem prompted suggestions by some to use force [the opposition party favored a hard-line on North Korea]. There were protests over the deployment of Korean troops to Iraq,

the readjustment of the ROK-U.S. Alliance, and the relocation of the U.S. Yongbyon Garrison. Many wanted national
defense reform and a projected takeover of wartime opera-
tional control that could no longer be delayed. Steps were
taken to ensure a security format to protect peace and the
economy. . . . Above all, the administration has put peace and
safety first, making its best effort to resolve the North Korean
nuclear issue peacefully and to manage inter-Korean relations
in a stable manner."

In June 2007, still filled with confidence, Roh went to
Guatemala City, Guatemala, anxious to win the bid to host the
2014 Winter Olympics. When Olympic Committee president
Jacques Rogge opened the envelope and announced "Sochi,"
Korean media networks were aghast. Many people were bit-
terly disappointed over Roh's failure. None could have felt
worse than Roh himself. Taking credit for securing the international Olympic Games would have been a tremendous bonus
for his presidency and a commendable way to leave office.
Instead, outgoing Russian president Vladimir Putin accepted
the victory.

KOREAN MISSIONARIES TAKEN HOSTAGE

A month later, 23 South Korean Christian volunteers were seized
by the Taliban as they traveled in Afghanistan. It frustrated the
government that the kidnapping was the cost of being seen as
a U.S. ally in Afghanistan, especially because it was unable to
draw on its Washington connections to free its citizens. The
kidnappers demanded a hostage exchange for Taliban prisoners held by the Afghan government or by U.S. troops. Afghan
president Hamid Karzai's government and his American back-
ers immediately rejected a prisoner swap deal that would only
encourage more kidnappings. The radical Islamic movement
responded by killing two male hostages.

President Roh sent a high-level diplomatic delegation
to Kabul, the Afghan capital, to request direct talks with the

After being held for five weeks in 2007 by the Taliban in Afghanistan, South Korean aid workers were released due to successful negotiations between the terrorist group and a South Korean envoy. Though unconfirmed, various news reports have quoted sources saying the South Koreans paid the Taliban a large ransom for their citizens, money that will likely contribute to terrorist operations.

Taliban. This led to the release of two sick female prisoners. Five weeks after the initial abduction, negotiators from both sides met with the International Red Cross and the Afghan Red Crescent Society and struck a deal. There was no mention of a prisoner swap. Suspicions arose that South Korea paid a ransom. But both sides denied any ransom. South Korea pledged only to honor a previous commitment to pull the country's noncombatant military contingent out of Afghanistan by the end of the year and to bar Christian groups and other nongovernmental organizations from traveling to and working in the war-ravaged country.

After all remaining 19 hostages returned home, Reuters news agency reported South Korea paid the Taliban U.S. $20 million. A senior Taliban official responded, "With it we will purchase arms, get our communication network renewed, and buy vehicles to carry out more suicide attacks." Later, an unofficial Afghan source reported the amount was U.S. $10 million, according to Reuters.

FLOOD CANCELS KOREAN SUMMIT

Humanitarian relief can be a powerful force in negotiations between opposing nations. In early August 2007, devastating storms caused deadly flooding in parts of North Korea. One-tenth of the country's impoverished farmland was destroyed. More than a hundred thousand people were driven from their homes by massive food shortages and loss of electrical power, leaving hundreds dead.

South Korea immediately sent $5.5 million in aid, including supplies of instant noodles, drinking water, blankets, medicine, and heavy fuel oil. The International Federation of Red Cross and Red Crescent Societies responded with another $3.7 million. Other northeast Asian countries followed.

The disaster came in the wake of a milestone summit between President Roh and North Korea's Kim Jong Il—only the second meeting between the countries' leaders since the peninsula was divided. But as summer flood waters continued to rise, the summit was cancelled. The North requested another meeting on October 2. Meanwhile, South Korea and China each began delivery of 50,000 tons of heavy fuel oil, and President Bush authorized $25 million in heavy fuel oil.

In rapid succession, Sydney, Australia, hosted a preplanned summit of the fifteenth APEC. The big news: North Korea will open its Yongbyon nuclear facility to inspection, and Russian and Chinese nuclear experts will shutter the North's nuclear program. Christopher Hill, assistant U.S. secretary of state and chief U.S. negotiator said, "Our plan is to get this done by

"ANYONE WHO BELIEVES PYONGYANG WILL ABANDON ITS WEAPONS BY THE END OF THE YEAR IS DREAMING."

December 31 and we need to have some nuclear experts get some eyes on, and we thought the sooner the better." Hill, who had been negotiating with Pyongyang since February, said that, under the deal, North Korea would fully disarm in return for aid and security guarantees, most notably the normalization of ties with the United States, according to the *Seoul Times* in 2007.

Richard Lloyd Parry, Asian editor of the *Seoul Times*, countered, "Anyone who believes Pyongyang will abandon its weapons by the end of the year is dreaming."

Following the APEC summit, Roh returned to Seoul to yet another scandal. In February, Hyundai chairman Chung Mon-koo was convicted of embezzling $110 million to set up a political slush fund. He was sentenced to prison, but an appeals court overruled. Judge Lee Jae-hong explained, "I was unwilling to engage in a gamble that would put the nation's economy at risk." Hyundai, the world's sixth-largest automaker, according to the judge was much more important to South Korea's economy than Enron was to that of the United States, the *Los Angeles Times* reported on September 8, 2007.

On October 4, 2007, President Roh, accompanied by an entourage of 200 officials, went to Pyongyang for a three-day summit with Kim Jong Il. Both leaders announced a joint declaration highlighting economic cooperation, pledged efforts for a nuclear-free Korean Peninsula, and agreed to replace the old armistice with a peace treaty formally ending the 1950–1953 Korean War. The armistice that suspended the war was signed by China, North Korea, and U.S.-led United Nations forces, but not by South Korea. A second summit would be held somewhere near the Korean Peninsula with China and the United States.

Both Kim and Roh agreed to open a direct flight between Seoul and Mount Baekdu, one of the North's major tourist attractions, to boost the lagging cross-border tourist business. "We are ready to launch tour programs any time soon," responded an official, who added that an airport near Mount Baekdu needs to be expanded before direct flights can take place. South Korea quickly shipped 8,000 tons of asphalt for paving a landing strip. The summit appeared successful, with other agreed points. North and South agreed to establish a special district in the North Korean west coast port city of Haeju and to set up a regular maritime transport service and a joint fishing ground. Both sides agreed to step up expansion of the Kaesong industrial park north of the heavily armed border where 44 South Korean firms are in operation. Other agreed points included resumption of regular freight train services between the South Korean border town of Munsan and Kaesong, repairs on the highway joining the North Korean capital and Kaesong, and refurbishing the railway between Kaesong and Sinuiju on the North's border with China. North and South Korea sent a joint cheering squad by train to the 2008 Summer Olympic Games in Beijing, China, joining Seoul and Sinuiju in the train line's inaugural run. As Korean news made international headlines, the North's prime minister, Kim Yong Il, scheduled a November visit to Seoul with his South Korean counterpart, Han Duck Soo. The announcement the world had awaited for six decades appeared to be on a fast train.

On December 19, 2007, opposition candidate Lee Myung-bak won South Korea's presidential election to become its seventeenth president on February 25, 2008. Yet Lee's sweeping victory came amid mounting public grievances over skyrocketing property prices, widening economic polarization, and rising unemployment. "Lee's victory will end a decade of liberal rule," reported the *Seoul Times* on December 20, "in which Roh and his predecessor Kim Dae-jung engaged in unprecedented

In the 2008 presidential election, conservative Lee Myung-bak defeated Roh Moo Hyun. Roh has relocated to Bongha, the village where he was born, to enjoy his retirement. Constantly distracted by the stream of tourists that pass by his house every day, Roh spends his time blogging, planting trees, and playing with his grandchildren *(above)*.

reconciliation with North Korea." Lee devoted a substantial portion of his campaign to accusing Roh of bungling management of the world's thirteenth largest economy and the home of 49 million people. Lee, the former mayor of Seoul and a Hyundai business executive, had been dogged by allegations of graft and financial irregularities. The pro-government United New Democratic Party, which nominated Lee's closet contender, and President Roh called for a special counsel to investigate the allegations.

"This was a verdict on Roh," said Kim Young-rae, a political science instructor at Ajou University, Seoul. "Voters appeared to have cast ballots out of spite for Roh rather than genuine favor for Lee."

In late October, the United States House of Representatives pressed Christopher Hill to explain a reported Israeli air strike on a Syrian nuclear facility under construction. The House Foreign Affairs Committee wanted to know about any evidence that North Korea was involved in spreading nuclear technology to Syria. Evidence of North Korean involvement would be grounds to void the pending nuclear deal. Hill responded that the Syrian issue had been raised in recent talks with the North but declined to say whether intelligence gathered as a result of the Israeli strike showed evidence to indicate involvement, according to the *Los Angeles Times*. Syria's envoy to Washington, Imad Moustapha said, "There are no nuclear North Korean–Syrian facilities whatsoever in Syria," reported *Newsweek*.

Perhaps the most damaging issue for outgoing President Roh was a brief statement from White House deputy press secretary Scott Stanzel: "The State Department had issued a declaration that North Korea had failed to meet the December 31 deadline established by its negotiating partners to disclose details of its nuclear weapons program."

When President Roh took office he established three goals: democracy for the people, a society of balanced development, and an era of peace and prosperity. Shadowed by hundreds of years of corruption and dictatorial rule, recent financial scandals, kidnappings and tragic incidents involving U.S. soldiers stationed in South Korea, a lost Olympiad, and anti-America protests, the president held to his vision despite being seen by some as mediocre. Like Abraham Lincoln, he maintained a firm and passionate belief in democracy and human progress.

There is no denying that Roh's leadership and democratic agenda helped forge the country's prominent position in world affairs, economic growth, and persistent efforts for reunification with North Korea. Despite his impoverished beginnings, he had risen to South Korea's highest office. Through years of tribulations and successes, Roh Moo Hyun remained unwavering in his dedication to democracy. History will determine his legacy.

CHRONOLOGY

6000 B.C.	Neolithic people arrive on the Korean Peninsula.
108 B.C.	China conquers the northern half of the Korean Peninsula.
57–18 B.C.	The Silla, Goguryeo, and Baekje kingdoms are founded.
A.D. 313	Korean forces drive the Chinese from Korea.
668	Goguryeo and Baekje are unified under the Silla dynasty.
918	Wang Kon founds Goryeo.
1170	Choe Chung-hon establishes military rule.
1259	Mongol armies conquer Korea.
1392	Yi Sŏng-gye founds the Choson dynasty, which lasts until 1910.
1592	Japan invades Korea.
1598	Aided by China, Korea drives out the Japanese.
1630s	Manchu dynasty invades Korea; the Yi dynasty rulers continue to serve as kings.
1642	Korea closes its borders to all nations; it becomes the Hermit Kingdom.
1785	Roman Catholic missionaries arrive in Korea.
1897	Japan forces Korea to open its ports and expand its trade.
1894	Demonstrations against the Choson government erupt into Dokdo rebellion.
1894–1895	The Sino-Japanese War.

1910	Japan annexes Korea.
1941	World War II breaks out in eastern Asia.
1943	In December, the Cairo Conference strips Japan of all land acquired since 1894.
1945	Japan is defeated in World War II. Soviet forces occupy North Korea. U.S. forces occupy South Korea. The Korean Peninsula is divided between North and South Korea.
1948	Syngman Rhee is elected president of South Korea.
1948	Kim Il Sung heads North Korea.
1950–1953	The Korean War.
1960–1961	Riots force Rhee to resign. Park Chung Hee stages a coup and imposes martial law.
1979	President Park is assassinated.
1988	Seoul hosts Olympic Summer Games.
1991	Both Korean nations join the United Nations.
1992	Kim Young-sam introduces political and economic reforms in South Korea. North and South Korea formally agree to denuclearize.
2000	Kim Dae Jung wins the Nobel Peace Prize.
2002	South Korea cohosts soccer's World Cup.
2003	North Korea continues its nuclear program in violation of the Nuclear Non-Proliferation Treaty.
2003	Roh Moo Hyun sworn in as president of South Korea.
2004	Roh Moo Hyun is impeached in March but reinstated in May. South Korea deploys troops to Iraq.

2005 Discord and conflicts face President Roh.

2008 In February, the presidency of Roh Moo Hyun ends.

BIBLIOGRAPHY

Behnke, Alison. *South Korea in Pictures*. Minneapolis, MN: Lerner Publications, 2004.

Breen, Michael. *The Koreans: Who They Are, What They Want, Where Their Future Lies*. New York, NY: St. Martin's Press, 1998.

Building Mutual Trust: President Roh Moo Hyun's Visit to the United States. Seoul, Korea: Korean Overseas Information Service, May 11–16, 2003.

Bunge, Frederica M., ed. *South Korea: A Country Study*. Washington, DC: The American University, 1982.

Cumings, Bruce. *Korea's Place in the Sun: A Modern History*. New York, NY: W.W. Norton & Company, 1997.

Dubois, Jill. *Cultures of the World: Korea*. New York, NY: Benchmark Books/Marshall Cavendish, 1993.

Harootunian, H.D. and Masao Miyoshi, eds. *Japan in the World*. "Archaeology, Descent, Emergence: Japan in British-American Hegemony, 1900–1950" by Bruce Cumings. Durham, NC: Duke University Press, 1994.

Hwang, Balbina. *Transforming the U.S.-ROK Alliance into a 21st Century Relationship*. Seoul, Korea: Korean Overseas Information Service, 2007, pp. 64–72.

Iriye, Akira. *Pacific Estrangement: Japanese and American Expansion, 1897–1911*. Cambridge, MA: Harvard University Press, 1972.

Kendall, David. *Korea Policy Review*. Seoul, Korea: Korean Overseas Information Service, 2007.

"Korea." *World Book Encyclopedia*. Vol. 11. Chicago, IL: World Book, Inc., 2004.

Kummer, Patricia K. *Korea: Enchantment of the World*. New York, NY: Children's Press, 2004.

Masse, Johanna. *South Korea: Countries of the World*. Strongsville, OH: Gareth Stevens Publishing, 2002.

Parks, Peggy J. *North Korea: Nations in Conflict*. New York, NY: Gale/Blackbirch Press, 2003.

Salter, Christopher L. *South Korea*. New York, NY: Chelsea House Publications, 2002.

Three Years of Participatory Government. Seoul, Korea: Korean Overseas Information Service, 2006.

Wallace, Bruce and M. Karim Faiez. "Deal is Reached to Free South Korean Hostages Soon," The *Los Angeles Times*. August 29, 2007.

Weimin, Chen. *Two Years of Roh Moo Hyun Administration*. Seoul, Korea: Korean Overseas Information Service, 2005, pp. 158–161.

Winchester, Simon. *Korea: A Walk Through the Land of Miracles*. New York, NY: Prentice Hall, 1988.

World Almanac editors. *World Almanac and Book of Facts, 2004*. New York, NY: World Almanac, 2004.

WEB SITES

The Asia Times
http://www.atimes.com/atimes/Korea.html

World Factbook—Korea
http://www.cia./gov/library/publications/the-world-factbook/index.htlm

Profile: President elect Roh Moo-hyun
http://edition.cnn.com/2002/world/asiapcf/east/12/19/skorea.new.roh.profile

Events in 1988
http://www.country-studies.com/south-korea/events-in-1988.html

Officials Expect Increase Violence in Iraq, says Rumsfeld
http://www.defenselink.mil/transcripts/transcript.aspx?transcriptid=3755

Events of 1992
http://www.fas.org/news/skorea/1992/920305-rok-usia.htm

Asia and the Pacific
http://www.heritage.org/Research/asiaandthepacific

Back Home Roh Met with Sharp Criticism
http://www.koreaherald.co.kr

The Roh Impeachment
http://www.jejutimes.net

How Dangerous is North Korea?
http://www.time.com/time/covers/1101030113/

North Korea-South Korea Railway
http://www.railway-technology.com

Korean History
http://www.koreaaward.com/korea/history.htm

Secretary Rice Meets with President Roh Moo-hyun
http://www.state.gov/r/pa/ei/pix/2006/74764.htm

Biographies
http://www.seoulsearching.com/

Joint Declaration on the ROK-US Alliance
http://www.whitehouse.gov/news/releases/2005/11/20051117-6.html

Test Runs, for Peace, Prosperity and a New Takeoff
http://www.korea.net/news/news/Newsview.asp?.serial_no=200070517030
&part=111&searchday=

FURTHER READING

Behnke, Alison. *South Korea in Pictures.* Minneapolis, MN: Lerner Publications, 2004.

Breen, Michael. *The Koreans: Who They Are, What They Want, Where Their Future Lies.* New York, NY: St. Martin's Press, 1998.

Dubois, Jill. *Cultures of the World: Korea.* New York, NY: Benchmark Books/Marshall Cavendish, 1993.

"Korea." *World Book Encyclopedia.* Vol. 11. Chicago, IL: World Book, Inc., 2004.

Kummer, Patricia K. *Korea: Enchantment of the World.* New York, NY: Children's Press, 2004.

Matray, James I. *Korea Divided: The 38th Parallel and the Demilitarized Zone.* New York, NY: Chelsea House Publications, 2004.

Salter, Christopher L. *North Korea.* Second edition. New York, NY: Chelsea House Publications, 2007.

Salter, Christopher L. *South Korea.* Second edition. New York, NY: Chelsea House Publications, 2005.

Worth, Richard. *Kim Jong Il.* New York, NY: Chelsea House Publications, 2008.

PHOTO CREDITS

page:

INDEX

About the Authors

SILVIA ANNE SHEAFER is an awarding-winning author, journalist, and photographer. Her previous books include the National Federation of Press Women nonfiction award-winner *Aimee Semple McPherson* in the Chelsea House *Spiritual Leaders and Thinkers* set and *Women in War*, a winner of the 1998 New York Public Library Young Adult award in nonfiction. Sheafer teaches in both public schools and community colleges. She is editor of the *International Senior Traveler* and travels frequently, writing magazine and newspaper travel articles.

ARTHUR SCHLESINGER, JR. is remembered as the leading American historian of our time. He won the Pulitzer Prize for his books *The Age of Jackson* (1945) and *A Thousand Days* (1965), which also won the National Book Award. Schlesinger was the Albert Schweitzer Professor of the Humanities at the City University of New York, and he was involved in several other Chelsea House projects, including the series *Revolutionary War Leaders*, *Colonial Leaders*, and *Your Government*.